William Cullen Bryant

An American Voice

WILLIAM CULLEN BRYANT

An American Voice

Edited by Frank Gado

in conjunction with
Nicholas B. Stevens

Antoca
Hartford, VT

distributed by
University Press of New England
Hanover and London

For **Olivia Alessandra** *and* **Greta Francesca**

in their childhood's merry days

Published by **Antoca Press**

1424 Neal Road

White River Junction, Vermont 05001

Distributed by University Press of New England

One Court St. Lebanon, NH 03766

Library of Congress Cataloging-in-Publication Data

Bryant, William Cullen, 1794-1878.
    [Selections.]
    William Cullen Bryant : an American voice / edited by Frank Gado,
    in conjunction with Nicholas B. Stevens. -- 1st ed.
       p. cm.
    ISBN-13: 978-1-58465-619-7 (pbk. : alk. paper)
    ISBN-10: 1-58465-619-0 (pbk. : alk. paper)
    I. Gado, Frank. II. Stevens, Nicholas B. III. Title.

PS1153.G33 2006
811'.3--dc22

                                                    2006025000

Contents

Prolegomenon

A friend once swore that the only prefatory information he wanted from an author was an account of how he had come to devoting so many precious, non-renewable hours to so ephemeral a result. Peter, wherever you are, this is for you.

Like most Americans of my generation, I first encountered Bryant while I was in public school. The anthology we used had three or four selections. I gave, at most, cursory attention to "The Yellow Violet," self-evidently the effeminate sort of poetry unfit for young males, and I quickly dismissed "Thanatopsis." Cool word, I thought, but the poem didn't speak to me: I preferred not to believe I would eventually have a rendezvous with death. The other one or two left no impression. I supposed the subject was a wood—or, as we said, "the woods." Living in West New York, NJ, the most densely populated square mile of town in the U.S. at the time, I loved the idea of a forest (though I had not yet been in one). But what the verse declared did not register.

After several walks through Bryant Park in back of the New York Public Library during my college years had done nothing to pique greater curiosity, I next read Bryant in graduate school. An unbearably dull course taught by a stunted giant in the profession required me to become acquainted with a slightly larger batch of Bryant's poems. To my astonishment, I discovered a kindred soul in the lines of "Green River" (a title I only later discovered referred to the river's name, not its color).

I started teaching in the mid-'sixties, just before campuses went mad. In a course I engineered about the American short story, one of my students asked what I thought of Bryant's tales. I corrected him. "Do you mean Flann O'Brien? The Irish writer?"

"No," he answered firmly, "William Cullen Bryant."

I smiled. "He was a poet. He didn't write tales."

Now it was the student's turn to smile–and walk away, clearly unimpressed by his teacher.

At the next class, the student arrived with a dirty, old anthology he had bought for a dollar at a second-hand shop. He opened it and showed me the tale, "The Indian Spring." On reading it that evening, I was so intrigued that I would include it in my course syllabus for the next three decades.

In the 1980's, as the editor of an academic press casting about for worthwhile projects, I decided to publish a collection of Bryant's tales. After initially seeking to consign the editorial essay to someone else, I undertook to write it myself. Before I could complete it, the operation of the press was "suspended," but as a consequence of my research, I presented a paper at a professional meeting. A friend from our graduate school years at Duke University, Kent Ljungquist, was in the audience. When, a few years later, he was preparing the *Antebellum Writers in New York* volume for the *Dictionary of Literary Biography*, he recalled my interest in Bryant and invited my participation.

The assignment offered a good excuse to visit the Bryant home in Cummington, a charming site in the Berkshires. By the time my tour ended, I had already hatched an idea. No book by Bryant had been in print for almost three-quarters of a century, and a small space off the entrance to the house would suit the purpose of a gift shop. Making a modest collection of representative selections available to the public struck me as a useful venture. A man who was not only a major literary pioneer but also one of the nineteenth century's most prominent figures in the shaping of America's profile was falling into utter neglect. In a very small way, I could mitigate this cultural shame. Moreover, profits from the sale of the book would contribute to the maintenance of the homestead, a treasure preserving a portion of the nation's past.

Within a month after mailing my *DLB* biographical essay, I began this book. The title came first: *William Cullen Bryant, At His Best*. It reflected my intention to show some unfamiliar sides of Bryant while also excluding the perfunctory poems that had not served his reputation well. Obviously, selection was the principal task. I called one of my closest friends, Nick Stevens, a retired military officer with an exquisite appreciation of the language who has been writing poems to please himself for decades, and he consented to help. Each of us would independently read through the Bryant collections and, in anticipation of arriving at twenty-five finalists, compile three lists: "Certain," "Negotiable," and "No." The results astonished us. From among over two hundred contenders, twenty-two of our top choices coincided. Just a single poem provoked disagreement: relegated to my third category, it perched loftily in Nick's first. (I relented: it's in the book.) For over two years, we negotiated the Negotiables, discussing, comparing, and wrangling until the implacable succession of second thoughts at last came to an end—a few days ago.

Inclusion of the two tales was always part of the plan, and adding two dozen pages showing Bryant's critical notions as a new American literature was coalescing seemed desirable. Whether I should myself intrude, and to what extent, was more problematical, but a short introduction to Bryant's life seemed appropriate, and I decided that supplementary critical appraisals of his literary contributions were excusable, given the paucity of such attention.

Originally, I meant to publish the book on my own so that my intentions would remained uncompromised, but on a whim one recent rainy afternoon I suggested a partnership in the project with the University Press of New England. Within a week, we had a deal. Working with Ellen Wicklum has been a delight. The only modifications our agreement produced were a change to the present title and substitution on the front cover of the Henry Trask Reilly painting for Linda Ide's superb portrait of Bryant. Felicitously, the portrait now graces the book as a frontispiece.

In addition to expressing my gratitude to Kent and to my faithful collaborator Nick, I want to thank Ellice Gonzalez of the Bryant Homestead for her patience, Jerry Loving for supporting my notion that Whitman owed Bryant a great debt, and Matthew Bruccoli for allowing use of my much-edited *DLB* entry on Bryant. My old friend Hank Reilly, whose sensibilities for nature are in the Bryant mold, executed his painting at the last minute, despite exigencies caused by his wife's death. Like all writers, I am indebted to those whom I importuned to read drafts of my essays: George Metes, John McElroy, and Pam Harrison. And to Doris Yates, who not only read my words but also put up with me while I wrote them.

FRANK GADO   *White River Junction, Vermont*

Sketch by Linda A. Ide

William Cullen Bryant, shortly after launching a literary career in New York City.

A Biographical Overview

No line of his poetry survives in the consciousness of his nation, and none of his editorial pronouncements still resonates from his five decades with the *New-York Evening Post*, yet William Cullen Bryant stood among the most celebrated figures in the frieze of nineteenth-century America. The fame he won as a poet while in his youth remained with him as he entered his eighties; only Longfellow and Emerson were his rivals in popularity over the course of his life. "Thanatopsis," if not the best-known American poem abroad before the mid nineteenth century, certainly ranked near the top of the list, and at home schoolchildren were commonly required to recite it from memory. At his death, all New York City went into mourning for its most respected citizen, and eulogies poured forth as they had for no man of letters since Washington Irving, its native son, had died a generation earlier. The similarity was appropriate: Irving brought international legitimacy to American fiction; Bryant alerted the English-speaking world to an American voice in poetry.

The shaping of Bryant's mind and personality owed much to his family circumstances in Cummington, Massachusetts, a small village in the Berkshire hills carved from the forest scantly a generation before his birth. His father, Peter Bryant, a physician and surgeon, had evidently chosen to settle in Cummington to pursue the affections of Sarah Snell, whose family had migrated from the same town in eastern Massachusetts; boarding at the Snell house, he won his bride. The couple quickly met misfortune. Whether because Squire Snell's relative affluence provoked the young husband to overreach when he saw an opportunity to become wealthy, or because his efforts to build a practice were failing, he joined in a risky business speculation and lost everything, including the humble, roughly-hewn cabin in which he had installed his wife and two infant children. Desperate—Cullen had been born within the year—he sought to recoup enough to stay out of debtor's prison by sailing as a ship's surgeon. That plan, too, proved ill-starred: the French stopped the ship at sea and Dr. Bryant was interned for almost a year in Mauritius. When he returned, he was forced to depend on his father-in-law's generosity to restore his place in the community. The birth of a third child, another boy, further squeezed financial prospects, and six months before young Cullen's fifth birthday, the Bryants resumed residence with Sarah's parents. Peter Bryant's letters to his own father indicate correct yet chafed relations with the patriarchal Squire Snell, despite the reestablished physician's financial infusions into the homestead as his fortunes improved. Adding a section to the house provided accommodation both for Bryant's medical office and for the four more children born from 1802 through 1807. The arrangement made possible some separation of the two households, but friction between the generations and their fundamentally different attitudes toward the world endured. William Cullen Bryant's reserve and his guarded nature throughout life undoubtedly were schooled by the familial constraints of his one home until he departed to practice law at twenty-two.

Years later, Bryant underscored that he was not among those who look back upon childhood as a happy period. The burden of farm chores, imposed as much for their value as moral discipline as for necessity, taxed his frail physique and delicate health, and although he was ever the prize pupil, eager to please by demonstrating his brightness, the district school imposed a strict regimen: lessons were taught under threat of the switch. Yet Cummington also offered bountiful compensations. An inquisitive child, Cullen learned to make a companion of thoughts stimulated by nature. The observations of plants and flowers, of birds and sky, and of brooks and rolling fields that occupy so much of his verse were trained by the boy's delight in investigating his surroundings. Social isolation fostered romantic sensibilities that would suit the evolving tastes of the new century.

The boy's grandfather pressed a contrasting worldview on him. Western Massachusetts in that period generally eschewed the liberal religious ideas that fanned out from Boston; its dour orthodoxies looked to the more conservative Calvinism of New Haven and the Albany area of upstate New York. Ebenezer Snell, a deacon in the Congregationalist church, studied theological writers and was as intractable in his interpretation of scripture as in his rulings as a local magistrate. In prayer services he conducted for his family every morning and every evening, he made certain that religious precepts informed the Bryant children's upbringing. Young Cullen first learned meter and poetry through the hymns of Isaac Watts, and he found an outlet for a love of language by constructing a makeshift pulpit of the parlor furniture from which he delivered sermons in imitation of what he heard at church. Worship stressed death and the power of the devil, and perhaps because of the boy's vulnerability to illness and chronic severe headaches, he pondered mortality, even at his tender age, and saw God's image as cast in a mold of fear and gloom.

The more compelling influence on Cullen's mental development, however, came from his father, a man of curtailed ambitions who aspired to being a citizen of a society well beyond Cummington's horizons. Peter Bryant, like his father before him, had chosen a career in medicine, and he became an early exponent of homeopathy; his passionate preference, however, was for the arts—for music and, particularly, poetry. As an erudite American, he had immersed himself in the ancients, a classical nurture reflected in his admiration for Alexander Pope and the other eighteenth-century British paragons of the Augustan style in poetry. Dr. Bryant also wrote verse, and if his derivative efforts fell short of distinction, they were nonetheless well-turned. When his precocious son began stringing couplets, Dr. Bryant took delighted notice. Although he held the boy to a high standard and was quick to derogate his exercises as doggerel, Cullen accepted his father as an expert mentor and took satisfaction in being treated as an equal. By the age of thirteen, he was seen as a prodigy. *The Northampton Hampshire Gazette* had published several of his poems, including a fifty-four line exhortation to his schoolmates he had drafted three years earlier. Beginning with patriotic invocation of the Revolution and concluding with a charge to "Keep bright mansions ever in our eyes, / Press tow'rds the mark and seize the glorious prize," it rapidly became a standard selection for school recitations in the region. If, given his age, the pose he struck in a poem composed in 1807 was patently absurd—"Ah me! neglected on the list of fame! / My works unnotic'd, and unknown my name!"—it nonetheless indicated his grand ambitions.

Ironically, an immediate fame beyond his imaginings awaited. Once again, he served as an extension of his father. When Peter Bryant, elected as representative to the state legislature in 1806, conveyed the political passions of Boston in his letters and his trips home to Cummington, Cullen absorbed the excitement, styling his juvenile understanding according to the father's Federalist partisanship. In 1807, President Jefferson led his Congressional followers to pass the Embargo Act, deepening the young nation's bitter division by party and region. The Act stipulated American neutrality in the hostilities between Britain and Napoleonic France, but the Northeast understood that neutrality clearly favored the French–and worse, that the bar to commerce with the British struck at the region's economic vital organs. At no time prior to the Civil War was the Union so threatened with dissolution. Dr. Bryant embraced the pro-British party's position, especially because his rationalist creed induced him to see menace in the embargo: an impoverished New York and New England, he feared, would be prey to Jacobin mob rule. Young Cullen, a captive of both his father's politics and his enthusiasm for Augustan poetry, fused the two in scathing verse. Addressing Jefferson as "the scorn of every patriot name, / The country's ruin, and her council's shame," he cited cowardice before "perfidious Gaul" and the rumors of a dalliance with the "sable" Sally Hemings as reasons for Jefferson to "resign the presidential chair" and "search, with curious eye, for horned frogs, / 'Mongst the wild wastes of Louisianian bogs." Dr. Bryant proudly urged his son to extend his efforts, and when the legislator returned to Boston after the holiday recess, he circulated the poem among his Federalist friends–including a poet of minor reputation who joined the father in editing and polishing the work. By spring, *The Embargo; or, Sketches of the Times, A Satire, by a Youth of Thirteen*, a pamphlet of a dozen pages, quickly sold out. A second edition–in which the 244 lines of the first swelled to 420, and, with the addition of other poems, its pages tripled–was published at the start of 1809. This precocious exhibition remained the talk of Boston, not only as a political weapon but also, a reviewer for *The Monthly Anthology* noted, as the earnest of a talent sure "to gain a respectable station on the Parnassus mount, and to reflect credit on the literature of his country."

The astonishing immediate response to *The Embargo* sealed Peter Bryant's determination to provide his son the humanistic education he himself had been denied. In the eruption of colleges across the young republic he saw an unmistakable sign that society would be drawing its leaders from the new elite being formally trained; nagging concerns about his financial resources and his precept that all his children should receive even-handed treatment would have to be pushed to the side so that Cullen's intellect might be properly nurtured. Dr. Bryant's notion that his dream of becoming a poet might find fulfillment in his son furnished a second, and psychologically more powerful, motive. Even an outstanding talent for poetry provided no livelihood, especially in America; a profession, however, would ensure his son the economic stability to permit development of his literary interests. And so, five days after his fourteenth birthday, Cullen traveled fifty miles to board with his uncle, a clergyman who was to tutor him in Latin.

The young man made swift progress. He had barely blotted "Translation from Horace. Lib. I. Car. XXII" before sending it to the printer during the first weeks of 1809 as one of the supplementary poems in the second edition of *The Embargo*. By the end of June, he had conquered Virgil's *Eclogues* and part of the *Georgics*, in addition to the entire *Æneid*. After a month's farming for the family, he enrolled in a school in Plainfield, a few miles directly north of Cummington. There he immersed himself in Greek from his waking hour to bedtime, and "dreamed of Greek" in between; at term's end in October, he could read the New Testament "from end to end almost as if it had been in English." The next year, except for a spring stay at the school to learn mathematics, he spent at home, expanding his reading in the classics, being tutored in French by his father, and acquainting himself with philosophical writers and post-Augustan British poets. The pace and range of his studies were not exclusively a function of his aptitude: Dr. Bryant, ever mindful of education's cost, trusted that his son's diligence, coupled with sufficient private study, would enable him to enroll at nearby Williams College in October 1810 as a sophomore, thereby saving a year's tuition.

The collegiate venture, however, did not survive the year. His most conspicuous achievement as a student, *Descriptio Gulielmopolis*, satirically expressed discontent with Williamstown and living conditions at the college; still more disappointing was the absence of intellectual zest among "pale-faced, moping students [who] crawl / Like spectral monuments of woe." The academic program offered little stimulation: only two tutors were responsible for instruction of all sophomores, and the courses were far afield of his interests. Obtaining an honorable withdrawal, he retreated to Cummington for another period of intense solitary study, this time aimed at admission to Yale that fall as a junior. Besides his "more laborious academic studies," he delved into his father's medical library, "became a pretty good chemist" by reading Lavoisier and performing experiments, and perused Linnaeus to gain a basic knowledge of botany. But then hopes for Yale faded. Dr. Bryant, reassessing the family's financial prospects and perhaps influenced by worsening health, concluded that money for the young man's future should be invested directly in a legal career.

Convinced he lacked the requisite eloquence and confident manner, Cullen was reluctant to accept a fate that condemned him to drudgery. Although he left for Worthington, six miles from home, to begin to learn the law a month after turning seventeen, his longing for Yale persisted. A letter to a friend records his distress: it speaks of farming or a trade, possibly even blacksmithing–an implausible option given spells of pulmonary weakness and his recurrent headaches–as preferable to the law should he not realize his wish to resume under-graduate studies in New Haven the next term. Even so, he was too much the product of his caste to ignore practical exigency: before the end of the school year, he committed himself to a legal career and strove to relegate literature to an ancillary role in his life.

This shift in attention was not altogether unhappy. Although Cullen had proved himself an assiduous scholar, he had much left to master as a young adult trying to determine his place in the world–and his two and a half years at Worthington may have been more instructive than college. If he only rarely excused himself from the rigor of poring over the black letter pages of Littleton and Coke to write verse, it is also clear that he more freely closed his books to enjoy himself. At seventeen and eighteen, he was discovering the pleasure of conversation at the tavern, and, with rising enthusiasm, of assaying the young ladies in the neighborhood's genteel parlors. Then, in mid 1814, he left the Berkshires for Bridgewater, the area of his family's origins, to join the law office of a congressman whose absences while in Washington required hiring someone to run his practice. Bryant profited not only from the legal experience but also from writing reports for his employer on the politics of his district–an exercise that served as a drill for his later newspaper work and forced him to examine the issues of the day independently of his father's Federalist views. Close friends noted his growing maturity. Bryant even contemplated temporary relocation in Boston to overcome his shyness by frequenting its courts and "engaging a little in the pleasures of the town to wear off a little of

[my] rusticity." But when his father declined to finance the experiment, Cullen, perhaps relieved that he would not have to pit his diffidence against the city's sophistication, stated that Bridgewater was sufficiently lively after all. When he concluded his training (having characteristically squeezed the usual five years to four), he was admitted to the bar in August 1815. A three-month respite in Cummington followed; then, within view of the front porch on which he had played as a child, he set up his law office in decidedly rural Plainfield. His youth had come to an end quite different from his expectations; dispirited, he wrote a valediction to "visions of verse and of fame." He had "mixed with the world" and sacrificed his purity; now he could only hope that those bright visions might "sometimes return, and in mercy awaken / The glories ye showed to his earlier years." He was all of twenty-one years old.

In fact, such poetic glories as he feared would smother under the workaday routine were in gestation. The prodigy who had written *The Embargo* and imitated the Classical writers was a skillful mimic of a mechanical concept of verse. Beginning in 1810-11, however, a surge of wholly new influences changed his understanding of poetry. Chief among these was *Lyrical Ballads*. His father had brought a copy home from Boston, perhaps because, as a devoted student of poetry, he felt obliged to acquaint himself with this boldly different address to its art and subject matter. Peter Bryant was not much impressed, but to his son, it was a revelation. Remembering the encounter many years later, he claimed he heard Nature for the first time speak with a dynamic authenticity: Wordsworth's language suddenly gushed like "a thousand springs." Quite probably, though, Wordsworth's full effect did not hit until some time after Bryant had begun studying law in Worthington. His mentor there, catching him scrutinizing *Lyrical Ballads*, warned against repetition of the offense, and Bryant, fearful of being sent away, steeled himself to obedience for a year. A vow of abstinence for the sake of the law, however, only stoked his desire to test his powers within the new possibilities Wordsworth had shown.

During the same period, Bryant also fell under the sway of the so-called Graveyard Poets. Henry Kirke White, virtually forgotten today, had a brief moment of great renown, though less for the merit of his lugubrious verse than for the controversy sparked by an attack on it in *The Monthly Review* and its defense by Robert Southey; White presently achieved martyrdom by dying, at the age of twenty, in 1809. Bryant no doubt felt an affinity with the ill-starred young Scotsman who had eluded his doom as a lawyer only to perish, it was said, from too assiduous dedication to study. Another Scotsman, Robert Blair, had an even stronger influence; his enormously popular 1743 poem, "The Grave," had marked a shift in taste and practice from the crisp wit and erudition of the Neoclassic age to the brooding emotional indulgence that would fuse with subsequent elements of romanticism. The direct language Blair marshals into blank verse pointed the way of Bryant's development; still more attractive was Blair's emphasis on acceptance of death's inevitability and overcoming the fear of extinction.

Mortality crowded Bryant's mind in 1813. Typhus, or a typhus-like illness, besieged the Worthington area that year. Several friends were stricken, but the suffering and death of a particular young woman plunged him into melancholy. In April, his best childhood friend had coaxed Bryant into supplying a poem for his wedding, even though it meant breaking his pledge to abstain from writing verse while studying law. Weeks later, the bride lay dying, and the groom again asked that "your lyre not be silent"; when she died in July, Bryant composed the first of his cluster of funereal poetry. The next month, his grandfather Snell, still vigorous despite his advanced years, was found cold in his bed. As the stern Calvinist had based his relationship with his grandson on obedience and respect rather than on love, the old man's death caused no emotional upheaval, but the sudden absence of such a commanding figure seemed to undermine life's earthly justification. The thought that all his youthful ambition for fame was destined to wither in the dismal light of small town litigation and deed registration resonated in this encounter with emptiness.

Bryant's belief in his grandfather's God had been deteriorating since before he attended Williams, where reactionary religious discipline was failing to repress forceful liberal currents. Peter Bryant's retreat from traditional Christianity exerted the greater influence, however: his devotion to the ancient writers reflected a humanistic view of life, which he transmitted to his son. When the elder Bryant's legislative duties took him to Boston, he became acquainted with the writings of William Ellery Channing and other early Unitarians and found them persuasive; although he continued to attend the Congregational church in Cummington, he refused to give public assent to Trinitarian liturgy, and a few years later he joined the Unitarian church. As Peter Bryant's closest intellectual companion, his son was profoundly affected by this departure from conventional tenets.

For a youth jarred by unexpected bereavements, the notion of a universe without God as a moral arbiter or of life without a manifest ultimate purpose was perturbing. Had his intended profession inspired ambition, he might have welcomed its challenges as a means of escape from dejection, but law offered him nothing more than the prospect of a living, burdened by wearying triviality. Instead, he turned once again to writing poetry, both to work through his discomfiture and to compensate for it. This reemerging poet, however, had little in common with the former prodigy schooled in the Ancients and in Pope's crystalline verse. The new Bryant, very much of his time, reflected the aesthetics and preoccupation with nature of the Romantics, coupled with the philosophical orientation of the Graveyard Poets. Once he had counted on his facility as the key to winning fame; now he wrote seeking clarity for himself. The pivotal poem, which he would substantially revise for much of a decade, was "Thanatopsis."

Relying on Bryant's casual recall, much later in his life, editors have frequently assigned the middle section–*i.e.*, the first of its several drafts–to 1811, speculating that it was begun in the early fall, just after his withdrawal from Williams. Indeed, a forested area at the edge of Williamstown was long known as Thanatopsis Wood because the poem had supposedly been begun at that spot. But neither the recollection nor the legend is supported by evidence. A better case can be made for 1813, when the stimulus of the Graveyard Poets was strongest; the notation of that year by Bryant's wife on the manuscript is more persuasive than the poet's aged memory. A third conjecture would advance it to some unknown month as late as 1815, when he appears to have been in a creative flurry. Whichever date one might prefer, however, the poem attests that its author was engaged in a daring effort to stare into the abyss and courageously pronounce his creed. The fact that the poem then lay unfinished for some years before its publication has occasionally been interpreted as a sign that Bryant was entering a long period of unresolved religious crisis, but the idea that a poet would transcribe a philosophical problem in carefully wrought meter only to suspend composition until he solved the problem is implausible on its face. Obviously, Bryant was reexamining his religious beliefs, but there is nothing tentative about the perception his poem describes.

During his eight months in Plainfield, Bryant evidently seized the opportunity to resume writing, refashioning his ideas and refining new aesthetic strategies in the process. Some of his very best poems emerged from this time. Even so, these were private delights, not steps in a literary career directed toward public acclaim. Indeed, he was careful to screen his poetic activities, lest the local inhabitants think he entertained lofty notions about himself or lacked a proper seriousness. Conscious of the need to adapt to the demands of the role he was determined to play successfully, he fought to overcome his inhibitions in public speaking and to cultivate the trust of potential clients. This strain to develop a facade that was untrue to his personal reality only heightened his sense of alienation. "In Plainfield," he wrote to a friend, "I found the people rather bigoted in their notions, and almost wholly governed by the influence of a few individuals who looked upon my coming among them, with a great deal of jealousy." By June of 1816, having despaired "of ever greatly enlarging the sphere of my business," he began investigating the prospect of joining an established practice in Great Barrington, and in October he moved to the Housatonic Valley town. But though the community changed, his inner struggle did not abate. What would not come to him naturally, he tried to conquer through will. In letters, he repeatedly resolved to defeat a tendency toward indolence and to focus on his legal work. This grinding determination succeeded; the following May, the firm's senior partner, recognizing the young man's keener industry and, perhaps, his superior ability, sold him his share of the practice at a bargain price. Bryant was acceding to his evident fate, but with obvious distaste. Responding to an inquiry from his former employer in Bridgewater, he confessed,

Alas, Sir, the Muse was my first love and the *remains* of that passion which not *rooted out* yet chilled into extinction will always I fear cause me to look coldly on the severe beauties of Themis. Yet I tame myself to its labors as well as I can, and have endeavoured to discharge with punctuality and attention such of the duties of my profession as I was capable of performing. . . . Upon the whole I have every cause to be satisfied with my situation.

Taming himself to the law's labors became all the more necessary when he decided the time had come to choose a wife. After the dearth of opportunities in Plainfield, Bryant's social life revived in Great Barrington. While his letters to former fellow law students pumped them for news of the lovely young ladies he had left behind in Bridgewater, he was scouting local entertainments; at Christmas time, he met Frances Fairchild, a nineteen-year-old orphan with "a remarkably frank expression, an agreeable figure, a dainty foot, and pretty hands, and the sweetest smile I had ever seen." By March, in writing a message of congratulation to a recent groom, Bryant worried aloud about his "many unlucky reflections" and feelings "of secret horrour at the idea of connecting my future fortunes with those of any woman on earth," but those very tremors attested the intensity of his desire to wed Fanny. And to qualify as a husband, he knew, would require paying less attention to the Muse.

A curious happenstance in Boston, however, would work to weaken Themis's hold. Peter Bryant's associations with the city's intellectuals had spurred an enthusiasm for an ambitious two-year-old publication, the *North American Review*, which, he wrote his son in June of 1817, should nicely serve as "the means of introducing you to notice in the capital." When the son ignored this prodding, Dr. Bryant seized the initiative. Taking some drafts Cullen had left behind in his desk and rewriting two others in his own hand, he submitted them to Willard Phillips, a friend of long standing from Cummington and an editor of the *North American*. Phillips in turn conveyed them to the journal's staff, which immediately perceived a remarkably gifted new American voice–indeed, Richard Henry Dana is reputed to have declared, in astonishment, "Ah, Phillips, you have been imposed upon; no one on this side of the Atlantic is capable of writing such verses."

The debut of this new voice, however, was clouded by confusion. Because the poems submitted were in two different handwritings, the editors assumed for many months following their September publication that they were the work of two different poets: father and son. And because the *North American*, like many journals of that time, printed its contents without identifying contributors, readers were unaware of the error, but a second mistake, consequent of the first, muddled the poet's intentions. Seeing that one group of poems bore titles while the rest, in Dr. Bryant's hand, bore none, the editors inferred that the latter constituted a single poem about death–to which one of them, drawing on his Greek, affixed the descriptive title "Thanatopsis." This sutured and misattributed version impressed the editors as the best of the submissions, but those identified as the son's from the start were also very well regarded. In December, the editors invited more submissions, and a month later, Bryant sent, via his father, a revised version of a fragment from Simonides he had translated while at Williams and a "little poem which I wrote while at Bridgewater," presumably "To a Waterfowl." Along with the poem written for his friend's wedding in 1813, these appeared in the March issue.

That Bryant offered no new composition, despite exceptional encouragement from the *North American*, strongly suggests that the magazine's readers scarcely noticed the poems. Certainly no hurrahs arose such as had greeted *The Embargo*; indeed, his debut in the *Hampshire Gazette* at the age of thirteen had caused more stir. But the approbation of the Boston literati would matter far more in the long run than a quickening of popular appeal. In February, Phillips, now engaged as Bryant's agent, suggested that he review a book by Solyman Brown as an excuse to produce a critical history of American poets and poetry, thereby establishing himself as the pre-eminent authority on the subject. Greatly aided by both his father's counsel and his collection, the twenty-three-year-old did not disappoint. The essay served not only as a cornerstone of our literary history but also as a thoughtful, temperate exordium to the many arguments for American literary nationalism about to erupt. A second essay, "On the Use of Trisyllabic Feet in Iambic Verse," published in September 1819, reworked material possibly first drafted when he was sixteen or seventeen and trying to shake free of Pope's Neoclassical cadence; even so, it did much to bolster his credentials as a scholar of metrics. That same month Williams College awarded him an honorary master's degree.

Meanwhile, Bryant had almost suspended writing poetry of his own. Edward Channing, the chief editor, recognizing his potential importance to the journal, had solicited a commitment "to spend a little time from your profession and give it to us." But Bryant's major allegiance continued to be to his practice. When he reached into his file and submitted "The Yellow Violet," Channing felt compelled to reject it because, without worthy companion pieces, it was too short to justify a poetry department. The following year, Bryant finished only "Green River," a skillfully wrought hymn to Nature, reminiscent of the earlier "Inscription for the Entrance to a Wood." It ends, ruefully, with the poet envying the stream, free to glide "in a trance of song," while he, bound to his office, is "forced to drudge for the dregs of men, / And scrawl strange words with the barbarous pen." A second poem, "The Burial-Place," contrasted the graves of England, adorned with symbolic plants of remembrance, with those of New England, neglected by the Pilgrims and left to Nature's vegetation, but this promising conceit remained a fragment, its development unresolved. Preoccupation with the conduct of his law office may not have been the only impediment. Death once again weighed on his mind–perhaps because he was enduring another period of poor health and his father was fast losing ground to consumption. His most sustained new project during the year was an essay, "On the Happy Temperament," which, contrary to what its title might suggest, scorned unbroken cheerfulness as a manifest- ation of insensibility. Yet its motive was not saturnine: Bryant was seeking to convince himself to accept death as an inevitable aspect of the mutability that lends "wild and strange delight to life."

In March 1820, Peter Bryant's lungs filled with blood as his son sat beside him, watching him die. More than a father, he had been a close companion and his most esteemed mentor; although his death had been foreseen for more than a year, Bryant deeply felt the loss. "On the Happy Temperament" had been an effort to prepare for the event, but "Hymn to Death," completed while he was in mourning, transformed the essay's probative speculation into a strange paean, launched as an intellectual celebration of Death's justice and equality. Once his father dies, however, grief causes the argument to collapse. Thoughts of the evildoers "left to cumber earth" affront tender memories of the father, and the injustice causes him to shudder at the hymn he has written, yet he refuses to erase its stanzas: "let them stand, / The record of an idle revery." Despite the enfeebling calculated ambiguity of its finale, "Hymn to Death" is more charged with passion than any verse Bryant would ever again write. Paradoxically, however, its anger cloaks a subtle movement away from the heresy of "Thanatopsis," particularly in postulating "a happier life" for his father after resurrection. (During the same months of the poem's composition, Bryant contributed five hymns to the Unitarian Society of Massachusetts for its new hymnal. Though still a nominal Congregationalist—who, moreover, continued to pay his tithe–he had rejected the core of Christian dogma, but these verses, while no more traditional than the Unitarian church, show him edging toward accommodation with conventional belief.)

Marriage in January 1821 to Francis Fairchild, the girl for whom he had written "Oh Fairest of the Rural Maids," lifted his sorrow, and a year later, almost to the day, Fanny presented him with a daughter, who was given her mother's name. Bryant's literary prospects also brightened. When a rift over succession to the editorship at the *North American Review* led Dana to resign, this dedicated advocate for the "new" Romantic poetry started his own publication, *The Idle Man*; even though the two had not yet met, Dana assigned a high priority to Bryant's participation in the endeavor. (Their correspondence regarding this matter initiated a close friendship that would last for the rest of their lives). Bryant sent four poems to the short-lived journal. "Green River," as yet unpublished though written the previous year, stands well above the rest. The thoroughly Wordsworthian "Winter Scenes" (later retitled "A Winter Piece") suffers from comparison to its model in tilting much more toward recollection than emotion; that notwithstanding, it is good enough to be mistaken for portions of *The Prelude*, which would not appear in print for another three decades. "The West Wind," the least of the group in both reach and achievement, moves a simple thought through seven undistinguished quatrains. "A Walk at Sunset," though it fails to realize at the end the extended meaning it has implicitly promised, reveals Bryant's evolving interest in the cycles of civilization, and particularly in the bearing of the Indian past on white American identity. That interest would soon become compelling.

In the spring, Bryant's boosters from the *North American* had persuaded Harvard's Phi Beta Kappa Society to invite him to read at the August commencement (incidentally informing him, to his surprise, of his election to membership four years earlier). Bryant accepted, overcoming his usual trepidation about public speaking, but instead of preparing an address, he chose to compose for recitation "The Ages," a poem of epic scope. A preamble of sorts raises Bryant's familiar questions about the meaning of mortality and obliquely alludes to his father's death—the echoes of "Hymn to Death" are quite distinct—but then, after a transition recognizing change as the way of all nature, the poem chronicles the march of civilization, age by age, to the discovery of the New World and America's realization of history's purpose.

The twentieth century judged "The Ages" harshly; even the poet's major adherents omitted it from their collections of Bryant's works. In the nineteenth century, however, when the idea of America's global

Manifest Destiny rallied much popular support, it fared considerably better. Bryant himself, despite his lessening regard for it in later years, continued to acknowledge its position in his public's affection by always placing it first in the six collections of his poems issued in his lifetime. 1821, however, was its ideal moment. American literature was showing its first signs of maturity, but it still missed a poet whose work could stand comparison with British rivals; "The Ages" nominated Bryant as that poet. In proclaiming a messianic America, Bryant implicitly built a case for literary nationalism as the means of expressing America's purpose: if "The Ages" was the necessary poem, Bryant was the necessary poet. The Boston coterie that had contrived for Bryant's appearance seized the moment. Before he left Cambridge, Phillips, Dana, and Channing had arranged for the publication of *Poems* by William Cullen Bryant, with "The Ages" at the front, followed by "To a Waterfowl," "Translation of a Fragment by Simonides," "Inscription for the Entrance to a Wood," "The Yellow Violet," "Song" (subsequently retitled "The Hunter of the West"), "Green River," and a corrected version of "Thanatopsis" with its new beginning and ending, revised during his visit. Sales were disappointing–a year later, it had yet to cover its printing costs–but reviews were good, not only in Boston and New York but also in England, where Bryant in little time became the only known American poet. In May 1823, while commiserating over dashed financial hopes, his friend Phillips could nonetheless rejoice that "the book has finally given you an established reputation."

Unfortunately, reputation could not provide for a wife and daughter or ease his obligation toward his mother and younger siblings since his father's death. Bryant was glad for his election and appointment to several minor political offices, including a seven-year term as justice of the peace for Berkshire County, to supplement his income as an attorney, but his grudging concessions to his profession would not subside. When a letter from Channing in June 1821 apologized for "soliciting literary favours" that would interrupt his duties, Bryant replied that none was due "to one who does not follow the study of law very eagerly, because he likes other studies better; and yet devotes little of his time to them, for fear that they should give him a dislike to law." For two years after he had completed "The Ages" and seen *Poems* praised, no alternative to reluctant fealty to his practice appeared possible. Then, in December 1823, came a bolt from the blue: Theophilus Parsons, the founding editor of *The United States Literary Gazette*, asked that he contribute "ten or twenty pieces of poetry," thereby joining "most of the best writers in Boston" in the new venture. When Parsons, politely apologizing, offered two hundred dollars per year for a monthly average submission of one hundred lines of verse, Bryant happily accepted. Well above the usual rate, the sum equaled approximately forty per cent of his annual law earnings.

Within a twelve-month period, Bryant contributed twenty-three poems to the *Literary Gazette*, seventeen under the terms of his agreement with Parsons and six more in 1825, when Bryant shed his commitment after a new editor, trying to economize, offered half the stipend for half the number of lines. As the necessity of keeping to a schedule would suggest, the quality of his submissions was highly uneven. "The Rivulet" is among the best of all his poems, but he had already written it before the contract with Parsons. Too much of what he wrote to quota reflects an impulse to supply appropriate embellishment for the magazine's upcoming number: e.g., "March," "November," "Autumn Woods," "Summer Wind." At times, the result is inspired, but in general the quality is mixed, and often an arresting image or a felicitous line leads into a cliché or a merely convenient rhyme. Even "To —— " (subsequently retitled "Consumption")–a sonnet composed in 1824 while his most beloved sibling, Sarah, lay dying–spoils a tender, personal expression of despair with a trite rhyme in a banal last line. Also, in awareness of writing for a magazine, Bryant may have begun to cater to popular taste. Despite having lamented a recent proliferation of Indian narratives, he fed the public's appetite with "An Indian Story" and "Monument Mountain," as well as another meditation on the displacement of one race by another in "An Indian at the Burial-Place of His Fathers." He evinced boldness by very few experiments with metrical irregularity, which had been one of his salient concerns. Two of the *Literary Gazette* poems are rhymed: "Rizpah," a Bible story in the vein of Greek tragedy, which Poe disparaged for the poet's "frisky" indulgence in a rhythm "singularly ill-adapted to the lamentations of the bereaved mother"; and "Mutation," a sonnet about the need to let agony pass and to accept death as a function of constant change. The third, in blank verse, was unquestionably his finest poetic achievement of the year, but "A Forest Hymn" represents more than a sure skill; it also shows the poet shifting in the direction of religious orthodoxy. Beginning, "The groves were God's first temples," it argues that the forest is an appropriate place for communion with God–not, as Bryant had previously held in "Thanatopsis," that God is immanent in Nature, or that the universe is the material manifestation of spirit.

Although Bryant was not consistently at his best, he had produced more poetry of high quality than any of his countrymen, yet he was still committed to a legal career. Then, in September 1824, an appellate court reversed a judgment he had won for his client; outraged that "a piece of pure chicane" should triumph over the merits of the case, he decided to quit the law. But this absurdity only precipitated a decision toward which he had been moving inexorably. Writing poetry at a steady pace for the Literary Gazette proved to him that he had not been disenthralled of the "dear witchery of song" after all. If, in itself, the stipend he earned was not sufficient, it showed that it might at last be possible to earn a living in the publications world. Perhaps the most persuasive motives, however, had to do with his reaction to Great Barrington. The town which had seemed so pleasant after the misery of Plainfield now irritated him with its provincial isolation and the pinched lives of its inhabitants. Friendship with the Sedgwick family of nearby Stockbridge increased that disaffection. Through Charles Sedgwick, a fellow attorney whom he had known at Williams, Bryant had met the other three brothers and their sister Catharine–all intellectuals devoted to literature. "The law is a hag," Charles wrote to his friend; "besides, there are tricks in practice which would perpetually provoke disgust." Two Sedgwick brothers lived in New York City and sought to convince Bryant to relocate where "any description of talent may find not only occupation but diversity of application." Meanwhile, Dana was growing concerned that Bryant, enmeshed in his practice and local political life, would "let his talent sleep."

A visit to Robert Sedgwick in New York almost a half year before the obnoxious court ruling had, in fact, already waked thoughts of departing from the Berkshires. Hobnobbing with the city's brightest literary lights, including James Fenimore Cooper, intrigued Bryant, and in February, he again visited the Sedgwick brothers. By spring, they were lending assistance to complex negotiations that would make him the editor of a merged journal, the New-York Review and Atheneum Magazine. Bryant felt liberated. On returning home to close his office in Great Barrington, he saw Charles, who reported to his brother Henry in New York that "every muscle of his face teemed with happiness. He kissed the children, talked much and smiled at every thing. He said more about your kindness to him than I have ever heard him express before, in regard to any body." Leaving his family in the Berkshires on May Day, the newly appointed editor hurried to New York to push the first number of his publication toward press.

Though unconvinced that he was suited to "sitting in judgment on books," Bryant applied himself to the task most creditably; however, the second part–*i.e.*, the "magazine," with its store of original works–presented more of a problem. The first issue featured a poem by Fitz-Greene Halleck, a New Yorker of rising reputation whose contribution, "Marco Bozaris," about a Greek revolutionary hero, advanced a popular, emotional cause to which Bryant had pledged himself while in Great Barrington. But little of comparable appeal was submitted for later numbers, and Bryant found it necessary to draw down his meager file of poems and then to try his hand at writing a tale, "A Pennsylvania Legend," in order to fill the magazine. Subscriptions, meanwhile, fell short of the publisher's hopes, and exactly a year after its launch, publication was suspended. But Bryant refused to accept defeat. For several anxious months, he had been making plans with a Boston editor to create an extension of the *Literary Gazette*, to be called *The United States Review*, and to merge it with a vestigial *New-York Review*. Ambitiously intended as a national publication, to be issued simultaneously in Boston and New York, it lost its first co-editor almost at once, and his successor, a Classics scholar working as a librarian at Harvard, quickly proved that the relationship with his partner in New York would not run smoothly. The first number appeared in October 1826; a year later, despite infusions of Bryant's poems and another tale, this journal, too, collapsed.

When Bryant had abandoned the law for a New York editorship, he said he was uncertain whether he was exchanging one "shabby business" for another, and after the failure of two journals, the second of which cost him an investment of almost half a year's salary, one might have expected regret over his choice. Instead, in spite of an onerous workload, it was proving a heady adventure. Upon his arrival, he boarded with a French family so that he might polish the language he had first studied with his father. M. Evrard insisted that he attend mass for his soul's salvation and tried to convert him to Catholicism, yet Bryant, respecting the man's ebullient nature and good heart, took it all in good stride, and when Fanny and their daughter moved to the city, they joined the crowded Evrard household for about a month. The renewal of his French had nearly immediate application: for the July issue of *The New-York Review*, Bryant not only wrote a long essay reviewing a new edition of Jehan de Nostre Dame's 1575 work on the troubadour poets but also translated Provençal poetry to accompany the critical evaluation. He did not stop there. Acquaintance with the famed Cuban poet José Maria Hérédia led him to learn Spanish and study Spanish literature, as well as to translate Hérédia's poems into English. Close ties with Lorenzo Da Ponte, Mozart's great librettist who had moved to New York from London and had made promotion of Italian opera his mission, introduced Bryant to this art during his first year in the city, while the busy editor studied Italian. Da Ponte published several works in Bryant's journal, including observations on Dante, and he subsequently translated some of Bryant's poetry into his native tongue. The cream of New York's creative artists eagerly welcomed the newcomer into their circle. James Fenimore Cooper invited him to join his Bread and Cheese Lunch Club, beginning an intimate relationship that would last until Cooper's death at mid-century. (Installed to membership at the same time were another poet, James Hillhouse, and Samuel Morse, a painter who would later gain greater fame as an inventor). "The Lunch," as it was known, became the hub of Bryant's social life. He had discovered in early adolescence a strong attraction to sketching; now, in the presence of artists determined to create a new age of American painting, that interest revived. In Thomas Cole, whom he had also first encountered through the Sedgwicks, he found a kindred spirit, and he made common cause with the other artists at The Lunch: Asher Durand, Henry Inman, John Wesley Jarvis, and John Vanderlyn. In 1827, the National Academy of the Arts of Design, newly formed by the group, elected Bryant its "Professor of Mythology and Antiquities." His literary friends at The Lunch and "the Den," a meeting room in Charles Wiley's bookstore where Cooper held forth, were equally prominent. Besides Hillhouse and Cooper, they included the brilliant conversationalist Robert Sands, whose long poem *Yamoyden* (1820) had begun the vogue for Indian subjects; the darling poet of the moment, Fitz-Greene Halleck; the estimable Knickerbocker and Congressman Gulian Verplanck; and James Kirke Paulding, who had recently published the satirical novel *Koningsmarke* (1823) and was the foremost advocate of a national literature. In addition, Bryant had come to know William Dunlap, both a painter and an eminent figure in New York theater. While in Great Barrington, on advice from the Sedgwicks, Bryant had aborted a political farce, his one attempt at writing for the stage, yet his interest subsisted. Through Dunlap, he served on two theatrical juries: one, in 1829, awarded a prize to *Metamora*, performed with distinction by Edwin Forrest; the second, in 1830, chose Paulding's *The Lion of the West*, which quickly became the most successful American comedy up to that time.

As both an American poet respected by Europe and an editor at the center of New York City's cultural renaissance, Bryant found himself called upon to play the role of prophet. Immediately prior to his move to the city, the *North American Review* had published his article about Catharine Sedgwick's *Redwood*. Initially intended to promote his good friend's novel, the essay developed into a rallying cry for an indigenous American literature—a cause perfectly suited to New York's expansive mood. The following spring, the man who had once worried about speaking in public was delivering four lectures on poetry at the New York Athenæum. Carefully reasoned and balanced, these pronouncements warrant comparison with Emerson's "The American Scholar" of a decade later as a charter for national literary achievement.

Only thirty-one when he presented his lectures, Bryant seemed the best candidate to realize the future he described, but a job he believed temporary and supplementary when he began it in July ordained a different course. Alexander Hamilton had founded the *New-York Evening Post* in 1801 as an organ for his Federalist party, but as the party weakened, William Coleman, the original editor, slipped from Federalist principles. An injury to Coleman in mid June of 1826, following a previous stroke that had cost him the use of his legs, forced him to rely on a substitute to help run the paper. Bryant was an obvious choice. Worried about the possibility of financial ruin, he had just obtained a licence to practice law in New York as insurance against calamity, but journalism posed a happier alternative. Moreover, his politics meshed with Coleman's, who had virtually become a Democrat. The young Bryant had ardently declared for protectionism in "The Embargo," but in his duties as, in effect, a Congressional aide while in Bridgewater, and then, more systematically, in Great Barrington, he had studied political economy and come firmly to the side of free trade. Although no document records the moment Bryant took control of the paper's editorial page, it is almost certainly marked by a sudden change to carefully reasoned briefs against high tariffs. Bryant had also been veering toward Democratic positions in other areas, and he admired Andrew Jackson and felt personally drawn to his good friend Paulding's good friend Martin Van Buren—all of which made for comfortable relations between the notoriously fiery Coleman and his assistant editor.

In October, despite Bryant's commitment to lead *The United States Review*, he accepted a permanent position at the *Evening Post*, and during Coleman's deterioration over the next three years, he assumed the title appropriate to the responsibilities he had been bearing: editor-in-chief. When Dana, his artistic conscience, warned that journalistic meddling in politics would stifle his poetry, Bryant famously answered that the paper would "get only my mornings, and you know politics and a belly-full are better than poetry and starvation." But Bryant's reply may have been somewhat disingenuous. The financial prospect with the *Evening Post* was alluring: Bryant bought a share of the paper and later added to his portion of ownership, confident it would make his fortune—as indeed it eventually did. More important, for all his protestations about having to "drudge for the *Evening Post*," politics fascinated him. In addition to liberal economic policies that included free trade, support for labor to organize, opposition to monopolies, pro-immigrant policies, and low interest rates, he consistently stood for resistance to the spread of slavery. In 1820, during a period when public speaking still frightened him, he had orated against the Missouri Compromise and denounced his senator, Daniel Webster, for brokering passage of such a morally repugnant law. As editor of the *Evening Post*, he remained true to that conviction, leading his readership in the direction of the Free Soil Party, and when that movement joined the amalgam that constituted the new Republican Party, Bryant and the *Evening Post* were among the most energetic and outspoken voices for its first Presidential candidate, John Frémont. Four years later, he was a principal supporter of Lincoln, and after the Civil War began, he became a forceful advocate of abolition. In late life, Bryant the editor and political sage had eclipsed the poet in the public's mind.

To see Bryant in the 1820's as having to choose between poetry on the one hand and journalistic politics on the other, however, is to imply too stark a divide. The New York of that time rather resembled the cities of Europe in its evolution of a cultural coterie, and Bryant had rapidly become one of its most prestigious members. Just as the literati associated with the *North American Review* had, however briefly, helped make Boston the nation's intellectual center, Bryant, as much as any other single figure, shifted that focus to New York. Poetic accomplishment accounted for a part of his influence, and his authority as editor surely weighed as much, but equally important was the conviviality which drew the city's writers and artists to him. Once diffident in nature, he had developed a knack for acting as a catalyst. Typically manifesting this quality were the three annuals and a collection of tales, all generated as exercises in camaraderie.

At the end of 1827, after the demise of the *United States Review*, Bryant, in company with Robert Sands and Gulian Verplanck, promoted the idea of a Christmas gift book similar to English annuals and *The Atlantic Souvenir*. Unlike its models, which were miscellanies by various authors, *The Talisman* would be entirely attributed to a single writer, Francis Herbert—in fact, a pseudonym for the three friends, each of whom assumed responsibility for about a third of the annual's pages while also participating in the work of the others. Two of Bryant's three tales for the initial *Talisman* seem to have been suggested by his collaborators. Recounting a purported Indian legend supplied by Verplanck, "The Cascade of Melsingah" resembles countless other specimens of the genre and is the weakest of the three. "The Legend of the Devil's Pulpit," probably suggested by Sands, has a rather flawed plot, but there is a sprightliness to the lampooning of local figures that appealed to readers. The best of the lot, "Adventure in the East Indies," a completely fabricated description of a tiger hunt, issued solely from Bryant's imagination; though a weak story, it is almost redeemed through creative invention of detail and evocative prose.

Despite the haste of its composition, *The Talisman for 1828* was well received, and the collaborators, who now formed the nucleus of the Sketch Club (also known as Twenty-One, for the number of members), developed a successor for 1829—this volume to accommodate other club members and to feature art work. Bryant contributed five poems, a translation of a Spanish ballad, and a travel account of Spain (which, like the East Indies, he had not visited), in addition to one tale of terrible cruelty and vengeance, "Story of the Island of Cuba." A final volume of the annual was compiled for 1830, even though duties elsewhere taxed all three collaborators. Again, Bryant's share in "Francis Herbert" was both varied and weighty: in addition to half a dozen poems, he wrote three tales. By now *The Talisman* had run its course, but a different publisher, Harper and Brother, thought enough of Bryant's collaborative approach to request another, similar collection in 1832 consisting exclusively of tales. Bryant was receptive. The birth of another daughter the previous June and the expense of moving to a new house in Hoboken, New Jersey, furnished sufficient reason to accept the Harpers' bid, but he obviously also welcomed the opportunity to write more fiction, especially as it meant working in enjoyable company with friends. To Verplanck (who withdrew at the last moment) and Sands, he added his editorial associate on the *Evening Post*, William Leggett, along with novelists Catharine Sedgwick and James Kirke Paulding. Supposedly stories told by visitors to the waters at Ballston, New York, *Tales of the Glauber-Spa* includes two by Bryant: "The Skeleton's Cave," a long piece evidently influenced by Cooper, and "Medfield," a moral tale, autobiographically based, about a good man guilty of one shameful act when he had lost his temper.

That Bryant never wrote another tale is conventionally attributed to lack of seriousness about the genre and to the poor quality of his efforts. But these explanations are misleading. To be sure, he was primarily a poet, and the first annual did have something of the character of a lark. Even so, his fiction deserves more respect than it has received. His first two tales, inspired by Washington Irving, may have been conceived by an editor pressed for material to fill his magazine, but they nonetheless express in prose the vision for American literature he outlined in his poetry lectures. "A Pennsylvania Legend," about an avaricious humpback who finds a cache of gold, imports the effects of European Romantic tales into an American setting; "A Border Tradition," a ghost story rationally explained, seeks to exploit America's rich variety of ethnic enclaves–in this case, the Dutch in New York. Had he thought little of these efforts? No such judgment has been recorded, but if he had a low opinion of his talent for such writing, it seems unlikely that he would have embarked on *The Talisman*, given its major emphasis on fiction. Moreover, the contemporary response to his stories was encouraging: all three volumes of the annual were critically praised, largely because of their prose, and the complete run of *Tales of the Glauber-Spa* sold so quickly that it was reprinted. Bryant's talent for fiction is nowhere more evident than in "The Indian Spring," published in *The Talisman for 1830*. Indeed, excepting only one or two pieces by Washington Irving, no previous American short story is its equal.

The signal literary event of the decade for Bryant, however, was his publication of a new edition of *Poems* in January 1832. At 240 pages, it added all poems published in the previous decade (plus five that he had kept in his file), and although relatively few of these were at the level of the best from the 1821 *Poems*, the greater number broadened the base of his achievement. The response acknowledged Bryant as "his country's foremost poet," and a British edition, shepherded to press by his friend Irving (who lent his name to the volume as editor, though not his services), was hailed as the work of the outstanding poet from the "primeval forest beyond the sea," worthy of inclusion among the ranks of the principal English Romantics. Later that same year, Bryant left his desk at the *Evening Post* to travel, first to Washington, then, after swinging through the upper South, to Illinois. His experience of the nation's great rivers, and then of the awesome sweep of prairie stirred him profoundly. The next year, he published his great blank verse poem "The Prairies," which in 1834 became the most notable addition to yet another edition of *Poems*. Bryant's trip bears comparison to Walt Whitman's pivotal journey to Louisiana and the Midwest in 1848: for both men, the experience of an America spreading boundlessly beyond their lives in the East affected their sense of voice as American poets.

When Bryant appraised his prospects after leaving Williams College in 1811, his passion for writing poetry appeared to be utterly without promise of a remunerative career. Except for Benjamin Franklin, no American writer had managed to support himself and his family with his pen, however meanly, and verse was patently an occupation for idlers. But in 1836, when the Harper brothers took Bryant into their publishing house, he was a most valuable asset. Numerous reprintings of his books spread his popularity still further, and the firm's generous royalty made him the richest poet in American history.

Unluckily, while his literary fortunes were in ascendence, sorrows battered his personal life. Robert Sands's sudden death in December 1832 deprived him of a dear friend, and the effects of political attacks on the conduct of the *Evening Post* during the following months exacted a still heavier psychic toll. As 1833 was closing, he looked forward to a respite in Europe with his family, and he began arranging for his friend Leggett to fill in for him at the *Evening Post*. At once, new vexations arose: William Coleman's widow demanded immediate payment from him on the mortgage she held for the newspaper, and the Jackson administration failed to make good a promised diplomatic appointment. When, amid raging abolition riots on New York's streets, the ship finally sailed for Le Havre in mid 1834, Bryant felt enormous relief, and he settled into lassitude as he traveled from France to an eight-month stay in Italy's cities, and finally to Munich and Heidelberg. Then news arrived that Leggett was physically and perhaps mentally ill; to save his investment in the paper, Bryant sailed for home, alone, in early 1836.

Only months earlier, he had been considering sale of his share of the newspaper and enjoying some ease, but Leggett so mismanaged its finances and drove off so many advertisers with his "radical" political stances that the returning editor had no choice but to immerse himself once again in its daily operation. National economic woes further hurt revenues, and the *Evening Post* did not regain its financial footing until 1839. But from that point on, it prospered, steadily increasing the value of his sixty per cent ownership, and its reputation grew as Bryant etched the faults of his political opponents with his acid editorials. What had supposedly begun in 1827 as a means of keeping his belly full now fed a modest fortune that, with shrewd investments, would eventually amount to an estate of almost a million dollars.

Financial stability made more active pursuit of his diverse interests possible. A lifelong homoeopath—he had been taught herbal medicine by his father—he published *Popular Considerations on Homœopathia* and agreed to head the New York Homœopathic Society at the conclusion of 1841. During these same months, he joined the governing committee of the Apollo Association (soon renamed the American Art Union); two years later, and twice thereafter, the organization tapped him to be its chief. In addition, two causes for which he had crusaded elected him to their presidencies: the American Copyright Club (which he addressed in 1843) and the New York Society for the Abolition of the Punishment of Death.

Public service was not permitted to exclude all other interests, however. The newspaper's demands on Bryant's attention and energy during the 'thirties had left none of either for poetry, but once the *Evening Post* was again profitable, he resumed writing verse. In 1842 he published *The Fountain and Other Poems*, all written after his return from Europe. That same year, he also signed an exclusive contract to sell his poems to *Graham's Magazine* at fifty dollars apiece–a record high price for poetry. After two years, most of these poems appeared as *The White-Footed Deer and Other Poems*, ten items in a slim paperback edition meant to launch the Home Library, a series Bryant and Evert Duykinck conceived to promote American writers. The poetry of his middle age, however, lacked the vibrancy of his early work. Two decades later, his final collection of new poems would prove a still duller echo of what was once genius. Published in 1864 for his seventieth birthday, *Thirty Poems* sealed Bryant's reputation as a Fireside Poet: augustly unassailable, yet fusty. One critic summed up his career by comparing him disadvantageously to the great poets of the age–Wordsworth, Coleridge, Keats, and Tennyson–yet he took care to comment that though the American could not match their idiosyncratic strengths, he was "the one among all our contemporaries who has written the fewest things carelessly, and the most things well."

Aware in his later years that his originality had ebbed, Bryant revisited the Classical magnificence he had loved as a youth. Translation, he explained, well suited careful old men. A selection from *The Iliad* in *Thirty Poems* hinted at what would be coming. In February 1869, he wrote his brother that he had completed twelve books of *The Iliad*, which were published the subsequent year. The next twelve, amazingly, he completed in less time than the first twelve, and the epic's second volume appeared in June 1870. Without pausing, he moved on *The Odyssey*, produced with similar alacrity over the next couple of years. In comparison, his original work was meager. Bryant brought out two revised collections of his poems in 1871 and 1876, but these were unmistakably memorials destined for the bookshelf's dustier reaches, despite a few new additions.

For the most part, the decades after he took a step back from the burdensome tasks of running the *Evening Post* were ceded not to poetry but to travel and the offices of a cultural elder. Resuming the European journey that had been interrupted by Leggett's debacle in 1836, Bryant returned to Europe in 1845. Leaving his family behind this time, he spent two months in England and Scotland, where he visited the elderly Wordsworth and virtually all the noted writers, then proceeded through most of the continent for the next three months. Upon his return to New York, however, he again had to deal with a problem at the *Evening Post*. Parke Godwin, a sub-editor who married Bryant's daughter Fanny in 1842, had strained relations with his father-in-law, probably because of the younger man's socialistic leanings. Also, Godwin had already begun a pattern of leaving the paper, rejoining it, and then leaving again. It had grown obvious to Bryant that, if he wished to be free to travel, he would have to look elsewhere for a trustworthy assistant. In 1846, John Bigelow filled that need, and in 1848 he became a partner in the firm.

The next spring, Bryant accepted an invitation from Charles Leupp, an art patron and Bryant's long-time associate in the Sketch Club, to be his travel companion. The two sailed to Savannah, then to Charleston, from where, after visiting Bryant's good friend, the novelist William Gilmore Simms, they embarked for Cuba. Ever since meeting Cubans during his early months in New York, Bryant had nursed a romantic vision of that Caribbean island, but his observation of slavery as practiced there, made more terrible by the execution of a slave before his eyes, shattered those youthful illusions. When he and Leupp returned to New York for seven weeks before sailing for Liverpool, he again glimpsed mankind's worst aspects. A rivalry between Edwin Forrest, a great American Shakespearean actor (and an intimate friend of Bryant) and an equally celebrated English tragedian attracted a mob, determined to drive the foreigner from his theater; this was bad enough, but then police and a unit of militia fired their guns into the mob, creating a massacre. Within a week, another horror began to swell with the first of over a thousand deaths from a cholera epidemic in the city. The two friends happily left these terrible scenes behind as they headed for Europe, and they spent delightful weeks in the Scottish remoteness. But once they left England, their jollity expired in a Europe everywhere menaced by a swelling militarism.

Shortly after Bryant returned in the fall of 1849, his old friend Dana urged him to collect the fifteen years of letters from his travels he had sent to the *Evening Post*. Published the following May, *Letters of a Traveller* scored a popular success, despite its cool critical reception.

Two years later, Bryant and Leupp were again off for Liverpool, then wended south through Paris, Genoa, and Naples before arriving in Egypt for a four-month exploration of the cities of the Ottoman Empire. Accounts of these journeys, too, appeared in the *Evening Post*, and in 1869, sixteen years later, were published as *Letters from the East*. One other travel book, *Letters of a Traveller, Second Series*, was set in motion by a penultimate trip to Europe, begun in 1857 when Bryant was exhausted after his efforts for the Frémont presidential campaign and fearful that the issue of slavery would rip his nation apart. In addition, his wife's health was giving him concern, and he thought the sun of Southern Europe might be beneficial. They were accompanied by their daughter Julia (who had learned Italian from her father) and one of Julia's best friends. Again they traveled to major cities, this time including Madrid, but the focus of the trip was Italy. Ironically, the trip that had been partly planned for Mrs. Bryant's health almost caused her death when she was stricken by a respiratory infection in Naples. For four months her husband cared for her himself with homeopathic treatment that he was convinced saved her life. After her recovery, the Bryants visited the Hawthornes in Rome, where the now celebrated novelist was writing *The Marble Faun*, and then again in Florence, where they also spent time with Robert and Elizabeth Browning.

As Bryant had feared at his embarkation in 1857, he returned to a United States in grave danger of dissolution and war. Once again, he poured his energies into electing a Republican president. He had instantly recognized Lincoln as a man of greatness when they met in 1859, and it was Bryant who introduced the Westerner to New Yorkers in the pivotal Cooper Union speech. After the election, however, Bryant criticized Lincoln for not immediately emancipating all slaves, and then for not prosecuting the war vigorously enough. The dispute taxed the editor, as did the managerial problems inherent in the doubling of the newspaper's circulation during the war years. The worst blow fell in 1866, when his wife died after a prolonged agony. To palliate his loss, Bryant made a last trip to Europe, taking Julia along.

Once back in New York, Bryant kept his title as editor, but the actual running of the paper steadily receded into other hands, and in the next decade his involvement increasingly became that of an investor protecting his stake. Even so, Bryant was a much-beloved and highly influential figure. No one could challenge his place as First

Citizen of New York. Among his causes over the decades, he had been the prime advocate for a unified and uniformed police department, agitated for the paving of the city streets, led the way for creation of Central Park, fought for establishment of the Metropolitan Museum of Art as a cardinal attribute of a great world city, and supported the right of labor to unionize. As a man of letters, too, though no longer consequential, he remained active. His last publisher, Appleton, aware that Bryant's name now guaranteed a handsome sale, asked him to write the text for *Picturesque America*, a two-volume folio of engravings that cost over $100,000 to print–a gargantuan sum in those days. Bryant agreed, though he soon wearied of the task of furnishing "the most tedious of all reading." The two parts were published in 1872 and 1874. A second massive project, *A Popular History of the United States*, was almost entirely entrusted to the pen of Sidney Howard Gay, who was then the managing editor of the *Evening Post*, but Bryant wrote the introduction laying out the history's scheme, with distinctive emphases on pre-Columbian peoples and on the deleterious effects of the politics of race on the nation's idealistic principles.

To the end, Bryant believed in physical fitness as well as mental exercise. A great walker, he insisted on climbing ten flights of stairs to his office instead of taking the elevator, and he made daily use of the barbells he had had crafted for him. Perhaps this very pride in his soundness made him vulnerable. At the end of May 1878, he spoke at the dedication of a bust of the great European and Italian liberal revolutionary Giuseppe Mazzini in New York's Central Park. The sun beat on his head during the long speeches, rendering the old man slightly dizzy, yet, characteristically, he insisted on walking from the ceremony instead of riding in a carriage. On reaching the door of a friend's home, he fell and suffered a concussion. A week later, a stroke paralyzed one side of his body, and he became comatose. Death came on June 12, 1878. At a public funeral, arranged contrary to his wishes, great crowds pressed in upon his bier. Later, a special train took the body to Roslyn, Long Island, his home for thirty-five years, where he was interred beside his wife. At the graveside, the minister recited excerpts from Bryant's poems about death, and schoolchildren tossed flowers on his coffin.

Selected

Poems

"They Taught Me,

And It Was a Fearful Creed"

They taught me, and it was a fearful creed
That God forgets his creatures in the grave
And to the eternity of darkness leaves
Thought and its organs. Fearfully upon my heart
Fastened the terrible doubt–and the strong fear
Of death o'ermastered me and visions came–
Horrible visions such as I pray God
I may not see again. Methought I died
And I was laid beneath the thick green grass
Of my own native mountains.–There were tears,
Warm tears, shed over me–such tears as fall
On many a humble grave, and dear hands wrung
In agony to think that I should die.
And all that I had learnt of virtue here
In the world's suffering–all that studious toil
Had taught me–all that from the book
Of Nature I had striven to transcribe
Into my mind–and from the laid-up thoughts
Of men of other days had now no place–
Parted–blotted out forever. . . . .

(Unpublished by Bryant, and left incomplete.)

Thanatopsis

To him who in the love of Nature holds
Communion with her visible forms, she speaks
A various language; for his gayer hours
She has a voice of gladness, and a smile
And eloquence of beauty, and she glides
Into his darker musings, with a mild
And healing sympathy, that steals away
Their sharpness, ere he is aware. When thoughts
Of the last bitter hour come like a blight
Over thy spirit, and sad images
Of the stern agony, and shroud, and pall,
And breathless darkness, and the narrow house,
Make thee to shudder, and grow sick at heart;–
Go forth, under the open sky, and list
To Nature's teachings, while from all around–
Earth and her waters, and the depths of air–
Comes a still voice–
      Yet a few days, and thee
The all-beholding sun shall see no more
In all his course; nor yet in the cold ground,
Where thy pale form was laid, with many tears,
Nor in the embrace of ocean, shall exist
Thy image. Earth, that nourished thee, shall claim
Thy growth, to be resolved to earth again,
And, lost each human trace, surrendering up
Thine individual being, shalt thou go
To mix for ever with the elements,
To be a brother to the insensible rock
And to the sluggish clod, which the rude swain
Turns with his share, and treads upon. The oak
Shall send his roots abroad, and pierce thy mould.
 Yet not to thine eternal resting-place
Shalt thou retire alone, nor couldst thou wish
Couch more magnificent. Thou shalt lie down
With patriarchs of the infant world–with kings,
The powerful of the earth–the wise, the good,

Fair forms, and hoary seers of ages past,
All in one mighty sepulchre. The hills
Rock-ribbed and ancient as the sun,—the vales
Stretching in pensive quietness between;
The venerable woods—rivers that move
In majesty, and the complaining brooks
That make the meadows green; and, poured round all,
Old Ocean's gray and melancholy waste,—
Are but the solemn decorations all
Of the great tomb of man. The golden sun,
The planets, all the infinite host of heaven,
Are shining on the sad abodes of death,
Through the still lapse of ages. All that tread
The globe are but a handful to the tribes
That slumber in its bosom.—Take the wings
Of morning, pierce the Barcan wilderness,
Or lose thyself in the continuous woods
Where rolls the Oregon, and hears no sound,
Save his own dashings—yet the dead are there;
And millions in those solitudes, since first
The flight of years began, have laid them down
In their last sleep—the dead reign there alone.
So shalt thou rest, and what if thou withdraw
In silence from the living, and no friend
Take note of thy departure? All that breathe
Will share thy destiny. The gay will laugh
When thou art gone, the solemn brood of care
Plod on, and each one as before will chase
His favorite phantom; yet all these shall leave
Their mirth and their employments, and shall come
And make their bed with thee. As the long train
Of ages glide away, the sons of men,
The youth in life's green spring, and he who goes
In the full strength of years, matron and maid,
The speechless babe, and the gray-headed man—
Shall one by one be gathered to thy side,
By those, who in their turn shall follow them.

So live, that when thy summons comes to join
The innumerable caravan, which moves
To that mysterious realm, where each shall take
His chamber in the silent halls of death,
Thou go not, like the quarry-slave at night,
Scourged to his dungeon, but, sustained and soothed
By an unfaltering trust, approach thy grave,
Like one who wraps the drapery of his couch
About him, and lies down to pleasant dreams.

The Yellow Violet

When beechen buds begin to swell,
  And woods the blue-bird's warble know,
The yellow violet's modest bell
  Peeps from the last year's leaves below.

Ere russet fields their green resume,
  Sweet flower, I love, in forest bare,
To meet thee, when thy faint perfume
  Alone is in the virgin air.

Of all her train, the hands of Spring
  First plant thee in the watery mould,
And I have seen thee blossoming
  Beside the snow-bank's edges cold.

Thy parent sun, who bade thee view
  Pale skies, and chilling moisture sip,
Has bathed thee in his own bright hue,
  And streaked with jet thy glowing lip.

Yet slight thy form, and low thy seat,
  And earthward bent thy gentle eye,
Unapt the passing view to meet
  When loftier flowers are flaunting nigh.

Oft, in the sunless April day,
  Thy early smile has stayed my walk;
But midst the gorgeous blooms of May,
  I passed thee on thy humble stalk.

So they, who climb to wealth, forget
  The friends in darker fortunes tried.
I copied them—but I regret
  That I should ape the ways of pride.

And when again the genial hour
  Awakes the painted tribes of light,
I'll not o'erlook the modest flower
  That made the woods of April bright.

"I Cannot Forget With What Fervid Devotion"

I cannot forget with what fervid devotion
   I worshipped the visions of verse and of fame;
Each gaze at the glories of earth, sky, and ocean,
   To my kindled emotions, was wind over flame,

And deep were my musings in life's early blossom,
   'Mid the twilight of mountain-groves wandering long;
How thrilled my young veins, and how throbbed my full bosom,
   When o'er me descended the spirit of song!

'Mong the deep-cloven fells that for ages had listened
   To the rush of the pebble-paved river between,
Where the kingfisher screamed and gray precipice glistened,
   All breathless with awe have I gazed on the scene;

Till I felt the dark power o'er my reveries stealing,
   From the gloom of the thickets that over me hung,
And the thoughts that awoke, in that rapture of feeling,
   Were formed into verse as they rose to my tongue.

Bright visions! I mixed with the world, and ye faded,
   No longer your pure rural worshipper now;
In the haunts your continual presence pervaded,
   Ye shrink from the signet of care on my brow.

In the old mossy groves on the breast of the mountain,
   In deep lonely glens where the waters complain,
By the shade of the rock, by the gush of the fountain,
   I seek your loved footsteps, but seek them in vain.

Oh, leave not forlorn and forever forsaken,
   Your pupil and victim to life and its tears!
But sometimes return, and in mercy awaken
   The glories ye showed to his earlier years.

Inscription for the Entrance to a Wood

Stranger, if thou hast learned a truth which needs
No school of long experience, that the world
Is full of guilt and misery, and hast seen
Enough of all its sorrows, crimes, and cares,
To tire thee of it, enter this wild wood
And view the haunts of Nature. The calm shade
Shall bring a kindred calm, and the sweet breeze
That makes the green leaves dance, shall waft a balm
To thy sick heart. Thou wilt find nothing here
Of all that pained thee in the haunts of men,
And made thee loathe thy life. The primal curse
Fell, it is true, upon the unsinning earth,
But not in vengeance. God hath yoked to guilt
Her pale tormentor, misery. Hence, these shades
Are still the abodes of gladness; the thick roof
Of green and stirring branches is alive
And musical with birds, that sing and sport
In wantonness of spirit; while below
The squirrel, with raised paws and form erect,
Chirps merrily. Throngs of insects in the shade
Try their thin wings and dance in the warm beam
That waked them into life. Even the green trees
Partake the deep contentment; as they bend
To the soft winds, the sun from the blue sky
Looks in and sheds a blessing on the scene.
Scarce less the cleft-born wild-flower seems to enjoy
Existence than the wingèd plunderer
That sucks its sweets. The mossy rocks themselves,
And the old and ponderous trunks of prostrate trees
That lead from knoll to knoll a causey rude
Or bridge the sunken brook, and their dark roots,
With all their earth upon them, twisting high,
Breathe fixed tranquillity. The rivulet
Sends forth glad sounds, and tripping o'er its bed
Of pebbly sands, or leaping down the rocks,
Seems, with continuous laughter, to rejoice

In its own being. Softly tread the marge,
Lest from her midway perch thou scare the wren
That dips her bill in water. The cool wind,
That stirs the stream in play, shall come to thee,
Like one that loves thee nor will let thee pass
Ungreeted, and shall give its light embrace.

To a Waterfowl

Whither, midst falling dew,
While glow the heavens with the last steps of day,
Far, through their rosy depths, dost thou pursue
　　Thy solitary way?

Vainly the fowler's eye
Might mark thy distant flight to do thee wrong,
As, darkly painted on the crimson sky,
　　Thy figure floats along.

Seek'st thou the plashy brink
Of weedy lake, or marge of river wide,
Or where the rocking billows rise and sink
　　On the chafed ocean-side?

There is a Power whose care
Teaches thy way along that pathless coast—
The desert and illimitable air—
　　Lone wandering, but not lost.

All day thy wings have fanned,
At that far height, the cold, thin atmosphere,
Yet stoop not, weary, to the welcome land,
　　Though the dark night is near.

And soon that toil shall end;
Soon shalt thou find a summer home, and rest,
And scream among thy fellows; reeds shall bend,
　　Soon, o'er thy sheltered nest.

Thou'rt gone, the abyss of heaven
Hath swallowed up thy form; yet, on my heart
Deeply has sunk the lesson thou hast given,
　　And shall not soon depart.

He who, from zone to zone,
Guides through the boundless sky thy certain flight,
In the long way that I must tread alone,
　　Will lead my steps aright.

"This Grassy Slope, This Ancient Tree"

This grassy slope, this ancient tree,
From infancy were dear to me:
Here, when the summer sun rides high,
Beneath these boughs I love to lie:–
The turf is cool–the shade is deep,–
And freshly here the breezes creep,
And, at the foot of this green hill,
The murmuring river welters still–
Look round–how lovely spreads the scene–
Gay meads and cottages between
And many a field where Zephyr strays
Among the rustling rows of maize–
Scarce forty years have passed away
Since waste and wild the prospect lay–
Here never had the hand of toil
Dared violate the virgin soil,
Nor echoing ax had ever here
Startled in deep brown dell the deer–
But Nature unreclaimed and rude
Reigned in this sylvan solitude
And listened midst her reverend groves
To the wild birds that told their loves–
The roar of winds–the solemn sound
Of water dashed from rocks around.

.   .   .   .

(Unpublished by Bryant, and left incomplete.)

Green River

When breezes are soft and skies are fair,
I steal an hour from study and care,
And hie me away to the woodland scene,
Where wanders the stream with waters of green,
As if the bright fringe of herbs on its brink
Had given their stain to the wave they drink;
And they, whose meadows it murmurs through,
Have named the stream from its own fair hue.

Yet pure its waters–its shallows are bright
With colored pebbles and sparkles of light,
And clear the depths where its eddies play,
And dimples deepen and whirl away,
And the plane-tree's speckled arms o'ershoot
The swifter current that mines its root,
Through whose shifting leaves, as you walk the hill,
The quivering glimmer of sun and rill
With a sudden flash on the eye is thrown,
Like the ray that streams from the diamond-stone.
Oh, loveliest there the spring days come,
With blossoms, and birds, and wild-bees' hum;
The flowers of summer are fairest there,
And freshest the breath of the summer air;
And sweetest the golden autumn day
In silence and sunshine glides away.

Yet, fair as thou art, thou shunnest to glide,
Beautiful stream! by the village side;
But windest away from haunts of men,
To quiet valley and shaded glen;
And forest, and meadow, and slope of hill,
Around thee, are lonely, lovely, and still:
Lonely–save when, by thy rippling tides,
From thicket to thicket the angler glides;
Or the simpler comes, with basket and book,
For herbs of power on thy banks to look;
Or haply, some idle dreamer, like me,

To wander, and muse, and gaze on thee;
Still–save the chirp of birds that feed
On the river cherry and seedy reed,
And thy own wild music gushing out
With mellow murmur of fairy shout,
From dawn to the blush of another day,
Like a traveller singing along his way.

That fairy music I never hear,
Nor gaze on those waters so green and clear,
And mark them winding away from sight,
Darkened with shade or flashing with light,
While o'er them the vine to its thicket clings,
And the zephyr stoops to freshen his wings,
But I wish that fate had left me free
To wander these quiet haunts with thee,
Till the eating cares of earth should depart,
And the peace of the scene pass into my heart;
And I envy thy stream, as it glides along
Through its beautiful banks in a trance of song.

Though forced to drudge for the dregs of men,
And scrawl strange words with the barbarous pen,
And mingle among the jostling crowd,
Where the sons of strife are subtle and loud–
I often come to this quiet place,
To breathe the airs that ruffle thy face,
And gaze upon thee in silent dream,
For in thy lonely and lovely stream
An image of that calm life appears
That won my heart in my greener years.

A Winter Piece

The time has been that these wild solitudes,
Yet beautiful as wild, were trod by me
Oftener than now; and when the ills of life
Had chafed my spirit—when the unsteady pulse
Beat with strange flutterings—I would wander forth
And seek the woods. The sunshine on my path
Was to me as a friend. The swelling hills,
The quiet dells retiring far between,
With gentle invitation to explore
Their windings, were a calm society
That talked with me and soothed me. Then the chant
Of birds, and chime of brooks, and soft caress
Of the fresh sylvan air, made me forget
The thoughts that broke my peace, and I began
To gather simples by the fountain's brink,
And lose myself in day-dreams. While I stood
In Nature's loneliness, I was with one
With whom I early grew familiar, one
Who never had a frown for me, whose voice
Never rebuked me for the hours I stole
From cares I loved not, but of which the world
Deems highest, to converse with her. When shrieked
The bleak November winds, and smote the woods,
And the brown fields were herbless, and the shades,
That met above the merry rivulet,
Were spoiled, I sought, I loved them still; they seemed
Like old companions in adversity.
Still there was beauty in my walks; the brook,
Bordered with sparkling frost-work, was as gay
As with its fringe of summer flowers. Afar,
The village with its spires, the path of streams
And dim receding valleys, hid before
By interposing trees, lay visible
Through the bare grove, and my familiar haunts
Seemed new to me. Nor was I slow to come
Among them, when the clouds, from their still skirts,

Had shaken down on earth the feathery snow,
And all was white. The pure keen air abroad,
Albeit it breathed no scent of herb, nor heard
Love-call of bird nor merry hum of bee,
Was not the air of death. Bright mosses crept
Over the spotted trunks, and the close buds,
That lay along the boughs, instinct with life,
Patient, and waiting the soft breath of Spring,
Feared not the piercing spirit of the North.
The snow-bird twittered on the beechen bough,
And 'neath the hemlock, whose thick branches bent
Beneath its bright cold burden, and kept dry
A circle, on the earth, of withered leaves,
The partridge found a shelter. Through the snow
The rabbit sprang away. The lighter track
Of fox, and the raccoon's broad path, were there,
Crossing each other. From his hollow tree
The squirrel was abroad, gathering the nuts
Just fallen, that asked the winter cold and sway
Of winter blast, to shake them from their hold.

But Winter has yet brighter scenes—he boasts
Splendors beyond what gorgeous Summer knows;
Or Autumn with his many fruits, and woods
All flushed with many hues. Come when the rains
Have glazed the snow and clothed the trees with ice,
While the slant sun of February pours
Into the bowers a flood of light. Approach!
The incrusted surface shall upbear thy steps,
And the broad arching portals of the grove
Welcome thy entering. Look! the massy trunks
Are cased in the pure crystal; each light spray,
Nodding and tinkling in the breath of heaven,
Is studded with its trembling water-drops,
That glimmer with an amethystine light.
But round the parent-stem the long low boughs
Bend, in a glittering ring, and arbors hide
The glassy floor. Oh! you might deem the spot

The spacious cavern of some virgin mine,
Deep in the womb of earth–where the gems grow,
And diamonds put forth radiant rods and bud
With amethyst and topaz–and the place
Lit up, most royally, with the pure beam
That dwells in them. Or haply the vast hall
Of fairy palace, that outlasts the night,
And fades not in the glory of the sun;–
Where crystal columns send forth slender shafts
And crossing arches; and fantastic aisles
Wind from the sight in brightness, and are lost
Among the crowded pillars. Raise thine eye;
Thou seest no cavern roof; no palace vault;
There the blue sky and the white drifting cloud
Look in. Again the wildered fancy dreams
Of spouting fountains, frozen as they rose,
And fixed, with all their branching jets, in air,
And all their sluices sealed. All, all is light;
Light without shade. But all shall pass away
With the next sun. From numberless vast trunks
Loosened, the crashing ice shall make a sound
Like the far roar of rivers, and the eve
Shall close o'er the brown woods as it was wont.

 And it is pleasant, when the noisy streams
Are just set free, and milder suns melt off
The plashy snow, save only the firm drift
In the deep glen or the close shade of pines–
'Tis pleasant to behold the wreaths of smoke
Roll up among the maples of the hill,
Where the shrill sound of youthful voices wakes
The shriller echo, as the clear pure lymph,
That from the wounded trees, in twinkling drops,
Falls, mid the golden brightness of the morn,
Is gathered in with brimming pails, and oft,
Wielded by sturdy hands, the stroke of axe
Makes the woods ring. Along the quiet air,
Come and float calmly off the soft light clouds,

Such as you see in summer, and the winds
Scarce stir the branches. Lodged in sunny cleft,
 Where the cold breezes come not, blooms alone
The little wind-flower, whose just opened eye
Is blue as the spring heaven it gazes at—
Startling the loiterer in the naked groves
With unexpected beauty, for the time
Of blossoms and green leaves is yet afar.
And ere it comes, the encountering winds shall oft
Muster their wrath again, and rapid clouds
Shade heaven, and bounding on the frozen earth
Shall fall their volleyed stores, rounded like hail
And white like snow, and the loud North again
Shall buffet the vexed forest in his rage.

"Oh Fairest of the Rural Maids"

Oh fairest of the rural maids!
Thy birth was in the forest shades;
Green boughs, and glimpses of the sky,
Were all that met thine infant eye.

Thy sports, thy wanderings, when a child,
Were ever in the sylvan wild;
And all the beauty of the place
Is in thy heart and on thy face.

The twilight of the trees and rocks
Is in the light shade of thy locks;
Thy step is as the wind, that weaves
Its playful way among the leaves.

Thine eyes are springs, in whose serene
And silent waters heaven is seen;
Their lashes are the herbs that look
On their young figures in the brook.

The forest depths, by foot unpressed,
Are not more sinless than thy breast;
The holy peace, that fills the air
Of those calm solitudes, is there.

Hymn to Death

Oh! could I hope the wise and pure in heart
Might hear my song without a frown, nor deem
My voice unworthy of the theme it tries,—
I would take up the hymn to Death, and say
To the grim power, The world hath slandered thee
And mocked thee. On thy dim and shadowy brow
They place an iron crown, and call thee king
Of terrors, and the spoiler of the world,
Deadly assassin, that strik'st down the fair,
The loved, the good—that breathest on the lights
Of virtue set along the vale of life,
And they go out in darkness. I am come,
Not with reproaches, not with cries and prayers,
Such as have stormed thy stern, insensible ear
From the beginning; I am come to speak
Thy praises. True it is, that I have wept
Thy conquests, and may weep them yet again,
And thou from some I love will take a life
Dear to me as my own. Yet while the spell
Is on my spirit, and I talk with thee
In sight of all thy trophies, face to face,
Meet is it that my voice should utter forth
Thy nobler triumphs; I will teach the world
To thank thee. Who are thine accusers?—Who?
The living!—they who never felt thy power,
And know thee not. The curses of the wretch
Whose crimes are ripe, his sufferings when thy hand
Is on him, and the hour he dreads is come,
Are writ among thy praises. But the good—
Does he whom thy kind hand dismissed to peace,
Upbraid the gentle violence that took off
His fetters, and unbarred his prison-cell?

Raise then the hymn to Death. Deliverer!
God hath anointed thee to free the oppressed
And crush the oppressor. When the armed chief,
The conqueror of nations, walks the world,

And it is changed beneath his feet, and all
Its kingdoms melt into one mighty realm—
Thou, while his head is loftiest and his heart
Blasphemes, imagining his own right hand
Almighty, thou dost set thy sudden grasp
Upon him, and the links of that strong chain
Which bound mankind are crumbled; thou dost break
Sceptre and crown, and beat his throne to dust.
Then the earth shouts with gladness, and her tribes
Gather within their ancient bounds again.
Else had the mighty of the olden time,
Nimrod, Sesostris, or the youth who feigned
His birth from Libyan Ammon, smitten yet
The nations with a rod of iron, and driven
Their chariot o'er our necks. Thou dost avenge,
In thy good time, the wrongs of those who know
No other friend. Nor dost thou interpose
Only to lay the sufferer asleep,
Where he who made him wretched troubles not
His rest—thou dust strike down his tyrant too.
Oh, there is joy when hands that held the scourge
Drop lifeless, and the pitiless heart is cold.
Thou too dost purge from earth its horrible
And old idolatries;—from the proud fanes
Each to his grave their priests go out, till none
Is left to teach their worship; then the fires
Of sacrifice are chilled, and the green moss
O'ercreeps their altars; the fallen images
Cumber the weedy courts, and for loud hymns,
Chanted by kneeling multitudes, the wind
Shrieks in the solitary aisles. When he
Who gives his life to guilt, and laughs at all
The laws that God or man has made, and round
Hedges his seat with power, and shines in wealth,—
Lifts up his atheist front to scoff at Heaven,
And celebrates his shame in open day,
Thou, in the pride of all his crimes, cutt'st off
The horrible example. Touched by thine,

The extortioner's hard hand foregoes the gold
Wrung from the o'er-worn poor. The perjurer,
Whose tongue was lithe, e'en now, and voluble
Against his neighbor's life, and he who laughed
And leaped for joy to see a spotless fame
Blasted before his own foul calumnies,
Are smit with deadly silence. He, who sold
His conscience to preserve a worthless life,
Even while he hugs himself on his escape,
Trembles, as, doubly terrible, at length,
Thy steps o'ertake him, and there is no time
For parley, nor will bribes unclench thy grasp.
Oft, too, dost thou reform thy victim, long
Ere his last hour. And when the reveller,
Mad in the chase of pleasure, stretches on,
And strains each nerve, and clears the path of life
Like wind, thou point'st him to the dreadful goal,
And shak'st thy hour-glass in his reeling eye,
And check'st him in mid course. Thy skeleton hand
Shows to the faint of spirit the right path,
And he is warned, and fears to step aside.
Thou sett'st between the ruffian and his crime
Thy ghastly countenance, and his slack hand
Drops the drawn knife. But, oh, most fearfully
Dost thou show forth Heaven's justice, when thy shafts
Drink up the ebbing spirit—then the hard
Of heart and violent of hand restores
The treasure to the friendless wretch he wronged.
Then from the writhing bosom thou dost pluck
The guilty secret; lips, for ages sealed,
Are faithless to their dreadful trust at length,
And give it up; the felon's latest breath
Absolves the innocent man who bears his crime;
The slanderer, horror-smitten, and in tears,
Recalls the deadly obloquy he forged
To work his brother's ruin. Thou dost make
Thy penitent victim utter to the air
The dark conspiracy that strikes at life,

And aims to whelm the laws; ere yet the hour
Is come, and the dread sign of murder given.

Thus, from the first of time, hast thou been found
On virtue's side; the wicked, but for thee,
Had been too strong for the good; the great of earth
Had crushed the weak for ever. Schooled in guile
For ages, while each passing year had brought
Its baneful lesson, they had filled the world
With their abominations; while its tribes,
Trodden to earth, imbruted, and despoiled,
Had knelt to them in worship; sacrifice
Had smoked on many an altar, temple-roofs
Had echoed with the blasphemous prayer and hymn:
But thou, the great reformer of the world,
Tak'st off the sons of violence and fraud
In their green pupilage, their lore half learned—
Ere guilt had quite o'errun the simple heart
God gave them at their birth, and blotted out
His image. Thou dost mark them flushed with hope,
As on the threshold of their vast designs
Doubtful and loose they stand, and strik'st them down.

. . . .

Alas! I little thought that the stern power,
Whose fearful praise I sang, would try me thus
Before the strain was ended. It must cease—
For he is in his grave who taught my youth
The art of verse, and in the bud of life
Offered me to the Muses. Oh, cut off
Untimely! when thy reason in its strength,
Ripened by years of toil and studious search,
And watch of Nature's silent lessons, taught
Thy hand to practise best the lenient art
To which thou gavest thy laborious days,
And, last, thy life. And, therefore, when the earth
Received thee, tears were in unyielding eyes
And on hard cheeks, and they who deemed thy skill
Delayed their death-hour, shuddered and turned pale

When thou wert gone. This faltering verse, which thou
Shalt not, as wont, o'erlook, is all I have
To offer at thy grave—this—and the hope
To copy thy example, and to leave
A name of which the wretched shall not think
As of an enemy's, whom they forgive
As all forgive the dead. Rest, therefore, thou
Whose early guidance trained my infant steps—
Rest, in the bosom of God, till the brief sleep
Of death is over, and a happier life
Shall dawn to waken thine insensible dust.

   Now thou art not—and yet the men whose guilt
Has wearied Heaven for vengeance—he who bears
False witness—he who takes the orphan's bread,
And robs the widow—he who spreads abroad
Polluted hands in mockery of prayer,
Are left to cumber earth. Shuddering I look
On what is written, yet I blot not out
The desultory numbers; let them stand,
The record of an idle revery.

The Early Anemone

Not idly do I stray
At prime, where far the mountain ranges run,
    And note, along my way,
Each flower that opens in the early sun,
Or gather blossoms by the valley's spring,
Where the sun stoops and dancing insects sing.
    Each has her moral rede–
Each of the gentle family of flowers;
    And I with patient heed,
Oft spell their lessons in my graver hours.
The faintest streak that on a floweret lies
May speak instruction to initiate eyes.

(Left unpublished by Bryant)

The Rivulet

This little rill, that from the springs
Of yonder grove its current brings,
Plays on the slope awhile, and then
Goes prattling into groves again,
Oft to its warbling waters drew
My little feet, when life was new.
When woods in early green were dressed,
And from the chambers of the west
The warmer breezes, travelling out,
Breathed the new scent of flowers about,
My truant steps from home would stray,
Upon its grassy side to play,
List the brown thrasher's vernal hymn,
And crop the violet on its brim,
With blooming cheek and open brow,
As young and gay, sweet rill, as thou.

And when the days of boyhood came,
And I had grown in love with fame,
Duly I sought thy banks, and tried
My first rude numbers by thy side.
Words cannot tell how bright and gay
The scenes of life before me lay.
Then glorious hopes, that now to speak
Would bring the blood into my cheek,
Passed o'er me; and I wrote, on high,
A name I deemed should never die.

Years change thee not. Upon yon hill
The tall old maples, verdant still,
Yet tell, in grandeur of decay,
How swift the years have passed away,
Since first, a child, and half afraid,
I wandered in the forest shade.
Thou, ever-joyous rivulet,
Dost dimple, leap, and prattle yet;
And sporting with the sands that pave

The windings of thy silver wave,
And dancing to thy own wild chime,
Thou laughest at the lapse of time.
The same sweet sounds are in my ear
My early childhood loved to hear;
As pure thy limpid waters run;
As bright they sparkle to the sun;
As fresh and thick the bending ranks
Of herbs that line thy oozy banks;
The violet there, in soft May dew,
Comes up, as modest and as blue;
As green amid thy current's stress,
Floats the scarce-rooted watercress;
And the brown ground-bird, in thy glen,
Still chirps as merrily as then.

Thou changest not—but I am changed
Since first thy pleasant banks I ranged;
And the grave stranger, come to see
The play-place of his infancy,
Has scarce a single trace of him
Who sported once upon thy brim.
The visions of my youth are past—
Too bright, too beautiful to last.
I've tried the world—it wears no more
The coloring of romance it wore.
Yet well has Nature kept the truth
She promised in my earliest youth.
The radiant beauty shed abroad
On all the glorious works of God,
Shows freshly, to my sobered eye,
Each charm it wore in days gone by.

Yet a few years shall pass away,
And I, all trembling, weak, and gray,
Bowed to the earth, which waits to fold
My ashes in the embracing mould,
(If haply the dark will of Fate
Indulge my life so long a date),

May come for the last time to look
Upon my childhood's favorite brook.
Then dimly on my eye shall gleam
The sparkle of thy dancing stream;
And faintly on my ear shall fall
Thy prattling current's merry call;
Yet shalt thou flow as glad and bright
As when thou met'st my infant sight.

   And I shall sleep–and on thy side,
As ages after ages glide,
Children their early sports shall try,
And pass to hoary age and die.
But thou, unchanged from year to year,
Gayly shalt play and glitter here;
Amid young flowers and tender grass
Thy endless infancy shall pass;
And, singing down thy narrow glen,
Shalt mock the fading race of men.

Summer Wind

It is a sultry day; the sun has drunk
The dew that lay upon the morning grass;
There is no rustling in the lofty elm
That canopies my dwelling, and its shade
Scarce cools me. All is silent, save the faint
And interrupted murmur of the bee,
Settling on the sick flowers, and then again
Instantly on the wing. The plants around
Feel the too potent fervors: the tall maize
Rolls up its long green leaves; the clover droops
Its tender foliage, and declines its blooms.
But far in the fierce sunshine tower the hills,
With all their growth of woods, silent and stern,
As if the scorching heat and dazzling light
Were but an element they loved. Bright clouds,
Motionless pillars of the brazen heaven–
Their bases on the mountains–their white tops
Shining in the far ether–fire the air
With a reflected radiance, and make turn
The gazer's eye away. For me, I lie
Languidly in the shade, where the thick turf,
Yet virgin from the kisses of the sun,
Retains some freshness, and I woo the wind
That still delays his coming. Why so slow,
Gentle and voluble spirit of the air?
Oh, come and breathe upon the fainting earth
Coolness and life! Is it that in his caves
He hears me? See, on yonder woody ridge,
The pine is bending his proud top, and now
Among the nearer groves, chestnut and oak
Are tossing their green boughs about. He comes;
Lo, where the grassy meadow runs in waves!
The deep distressful silence of the scene
Breaks up with mingling of unnumbered sounds
And universal motion. He is come,
Shaking a shower of blossoms from the shrubs,

And bearing on their fragrance; and he brings
Music of birds, and rustling of young boughs,
And sound of swaying branches, and the voice
Of distant waterfalls. All the green herbs
Are stirring in his breath; a thousand flowers,
By the road-side and the borders of the brook,
Nod gayly to each other; glossy leaves
Are twinkling in the sun, as if the dew
Were on them yet, and silver waters break
Into small waves and sparkle as he comes.

Love's Seasons

Dost thou idly ask to hear
  At what gentle seasons
Nymphs relent, when lovers near
  Press the tenderest reasons?
Ah, they give their faith too oft
  To the careless wooer;
Maidens' hearts are always soft:
  Would that men's were truer!

Woo the fair one when around
  Early birds are singing;
When, o'er all the fragrant ground,
  Early herbs are springing;
When the brookside, bank, and grove,
  All with blossoms laden,
Shine with beauty, breathe of love,–
  Woo the timid maiden.

Woo her when, with rosy blush,
  Summer eve is sinking;
When, on rills that softly gush,
  Stars are softly winking;
When through boughs that knit the bower
  Moonlight gleams are stealing;
Woo her, till the gentle hour
  Wake a gentler feeling.

Woo her, when autumnal dyes
  Tinge the woody mountain;
When the dropping foliage lies
  In the weedy fountain;
Let the scene, that tells how fast
  Youth is passing over,
Warn her, ere her bloom is past,
  To secure her lover.

Woo her when the north winds call
  At the lattice nightly;
When, within the cheerful hall,
  Blaze the fagots brightly;
While the wintry tempest round
  Sweeps the landscape hoary,
Sweeter in her ear shall sound
  Love's delightful story.

Mutation

They talk of short-lived pleasure—be it so—
   Pain dies as quickly: stern, hard-featured pain
Expires, and lets her weary prisoner go.
   The fiercest agonies have shortest reign;
   And after dreams of horror, comes again
The welcome morning with its rays of peace.
   Oblivion, softly wiping out the stain,
Makes the strong secret pangs of shame to cease:
Remorse is virtue's root; its fair increase
   Are fruits of innocence and blessedness:
Thus joy, o'erborne and bound, doth still release
   His young limbs from the chains that round him press.
Weep not that the world changes—did it keep
A stable, changeless state, 'twere cause indeed to weep.

To a Mosquito

Fair insect! that, with threadlike legs spread out,
   And blood-extracting bill and filmy wing,
Dost murmur, as thou slowly sail'st about,
   In pitiless ears full many a plaintive thing,
And tell how little our large veins would bleed,
Would we but yield them to thy bitter need.

Unwillingly, I own, and, what is worse,
   Full angrily men hearken to thy plaint;
Thou gettest many a brush, and many a curse,
   For saying thou art gaunt, and starved, and faint;
Even the old beggar, while he asks for food,
Would kill thee, hapless stranger, if he could.

I call thee stranger, for the town, I ween,
   Has not the honor of so proud a birth,–
Thou com'st from Jersey meadows, fresh and green,
   The offspring of the gods, though born on earth;
For Titan was thy sire, and fair was she,
The ocean-nymph that nursed thy infancy.

Beneath the rushes was thy cradle swung,
   And when at length thy gauzy wings grew strong,
Abroad to gentle airs their folds were flung,
   Rose in the sky and bore thee soft along;
The south wind breathed to waft thee on thy way,
And danced and shone beneath the billowy bay.

Calm rose afar the city spires, and thence
   Came the deep murmur of its throng of men,
And as its grateful odors met thy sense,
   They seemed the perfumes of thy native fen.
Fair lay its crowded streets, and at the sight
Thy tiny song grew shriller with delight.

At length thy pinions fluttered in Broadway–
   Ah! there were fairy steps, and white necks kissed
By wanton airs, and eyes whose killing ray
   Shone through the snowy veils like stars through mist;
And fresh as morn, on many a cheek and chin,
Bloomed the bright blood through the transparent skin.

Sure these were sights to touch an anchorite!
    What! do I hear thy slender voice complain?
Thou wailest when I talk of beauty's light,
    As if it brought the memory of pain;
Thou art a wayward being–well–come near,
And pour thy tale of sorrow in my ear.

What sayest thou–slanderer! –rouge makes thee sick?
    And China bloom at best is sorry food?
And Rowland's Kalydor, if laid on thick,
    Poisons the thirsty wretch that bores for blood?
Go! 'twas a just reward that met thy crime–
But shun the sacrilege another time.

That bloom was made to look at, not to touch;
    To worship, not approach, that radiant white;
And well might sudden vengeance light on such
    As dared, like thee, most impiously to bite.
Thou shouldst have gazed at distance and admired,
Murmured thy adoration, and retired.

Thou'rt welcome to the town; but why come here
    To bleed a brother poet, gaunt like thee?
Alas! the little blood I have is dear,
    And thin will he the banquet drawn from me.
Look round–the pale-eyed sisters in my cell,
Thy old acquaintance, Song and Famine, dwell.

Try some plump alderman, and suck the blood
    Enriched by generous wine and costly meat;
On well-filled skins, sleek as thy native mud,
    Fix thy light pump and press thy freckled feet.
Go to the men for whom, in ocean's halls,
The oyster breeds, and the green turtle sprawls.

There corks are drawn, and the red vintage flows
    To fill the swelling veins for thee, and now
The ruddy cheek and now the ruddier nose
    Shall tempt thee, as thou flittest round the brow.
And when the hour of sleep its quiet brings,
No angry hands shall rise to brush thy wings.

A Scene on the Banks of the Hudson

Cool shades and dews are round my way,
And silence of the early day;
Mid the dark rocks that watch his bed,
Glitters the mighty Hudson spread,
Unrippled, save by drops that fall
From shrubs that fringe his mountain wall;
And o'er the clear still water swells
The music of the Sabbath bells.

All, save this little nook of land,
Circled with trees, on which I stand;
All, save that line of hills which lie
Suspended in the mimic sky–
Seems a blue void, above, below,
Through which the white clouds come and go;
And from the green world's farthest steep
I gaze into the airy deep.

Loveliest of lovely things are they,
On earth, that soonest pass away.
The rose that lives its little hour
Is prized beyond the sculptured flower.
Even love, long tried and cherished long,
Becomes more tender and more strong
At thought of that insatiate grave
From which its yearnings cannot save.

River! in this still hour thou hast
Too much of heaven on earth to last;
Nor long may thy still waters lie,
An image of the glorious sky.
Thy fate and mine are not repose,
And ere another evening close,
Thou to thy tides shalt turn again,
And I to seek the crowd of men.

"I Broke the Spell That Held Me Long"

I broke the spell that held me long,
The dear, dear witchery of song.
I said, the poet's idle lore
Shall waste my prime of years no more,
For Poetry, though heavenly born,
Consorts with poverty and scorn.

I broke the spell–nor deemed its power
Could fetter me another hour.
Ah, thoughtless! how could I forget
Its causes were around me yet?
For wheresoe'er I looked, the while,
Was Nature's everlasting smile.

Still came and lingered on my sight
Of flowers and streams the bloom and light,
And glory of the stars and sun; –
And these and poetry are one.
They, ere the world had held me long,
Recalled me to the love of song.

October

Ay, thou art welcome, heaven's delicious breath!
    When woods begin to wear the crimson leaf,
    And suns grow meek, and the meek suns grow brief,
And the year smiles as it draws near its death.
Wind of the sunny south! oh, still delay
    In the gay woods and in the golden air,
    Like to a good old age released from care,
Journeying, in long serenity, away.
In such a bright, late quiet, would that I
    Might wear out life like thee, mid bowers and brooks,
    And, dearer yet, the sunshine of kind looks,
And music of kind voices ever nigh,
And when my last sand twinkled in the glass,
Pass silently from men, as thou dost pass.

A Forest Hymn

The groves were God's first temples. Ere man learned
To hew the shaft, and lay the architrave,
And spread the roof above them–ere he framed
The lofty vault, to gather and roll back
The sound of anthems; in the darkling wood,
Amid the cool and silence, he knelt down,
And offered to the Mightiest solemn thanks
And supplication. For his simple heart
Might not resist the sacred influences
Which, from the stilly twilight of the place,
And from the gray old trunks that high in heaven
Mingled their mossy boughs, and from the sound
Of the invisible breath that swayed at once
All their green tops, stole over him, and bowed
His spirit with the thought of boundless power
And inaccessible majesty. Ah, why
Should we, in the world's riper years, neglect
God's ancient sanctuaries, and adore
Only among the crowd, and under roofs
That our frail hands have raised? Let me, at least,
Here, in the shadow of this aged wood,
Offer one hymn–thrice happy, if it find
Acceptance in His ear.
     Father, thy hand
Hath reared these venerable columns; thou
Didst weave this verdant roof. Thou didst look down
Upon the naked earth, and, forthwith, rose
All these fair ranks of trees. They, in thy sun,
Budded, and shook their green leaves in thy breeze,
And shot toward heaven. The century-living crow
Whose birth was in their tops, grew old and died
Among their branches, till, at last, they stood,
As now they stand, massy, and tall, and dark,
Fit shrine for humble worshipper to hold
Communion with his Maker. These dim vaults,
These winding aisles, of human pomp or pride

Report not. No fantastic carvings show
The boast of our vain race to change the form
Of thy fair works. But thou art here—thou fill'st
The solitude. Thou art in the soft winds
That run along the summit of these trees
In music; thou art in the cooler breath
That from the inmost darkness of the place
Comes, scarcely felt; the barky trunks, the ground,
The fresh moist ground, are all instinct with thee.
Here is continual worship;—Nature, here,
In the tranquillity that thou dost love,
Enjoys thy presence. Noiselessly, around,
From perch to perch, the solitary bird
Passes; and yon clear spring, that, midst its herbs,
Wells softly forth and wandering steeps the roots
Of half the mighty forest, tells no tale
Of all the good it does. Thou hast not left
Thyself without a witness, in these shades,
Of thy perfections. Grandeur, strength, and grace
Are here to speak of thee. This mighty oak—
By whose immovable stem I stand and seem
Almost annihilated—not a prince,
In all that proud old world beyond the deep,
E'er wore his crown as loftily as he
Wears the green coronal of leaves with which
Thy hand has graced him. Nestled at his root
Is beauty, such as blooms not in the glare
Of the broad sun. That delicate forest flower,
With scented breath and look so like a smile,
Seems, as it issues from the shapeless mould,
An emanation of the indwelling Life,
A visible token of the upholding Love,
That are the soul of this great universe.

   My heart is awed within me when I think
Of the great miracle that still goes on,
In silence, round me—the perpetual work
Of thy creation, finished, yet renewed

Forever. Written on thy works I read
The lesson of thy own eternity.
Lo! all grow old and die—but see again,
How on the faltering footsteps of decay
Youth presses—ever gay and beautiful youth
In all its beautiful forms. These lofty trees
Wave not less proudly that their ancestors
Moulder beneath them. Oh, there is not lost
One of earth's charms: upon her bosom yet,
After the flight of untold centuries,
The freshness of her far beginning lies
And yet shall lie. Life mocks the idle hate
Of his arch-enemy Death—yea, seats himself
Upon the tyrant's throne—the sepulchre,
And of the triumphs of his ghastly foe
Makes his own nourishment. For he came forth
From thine own bosom, and shall have no end.

There have been holy men who hid themselves
Deep in the woody wilderness, and gave
Their lives to thought and prayer, till they outlived
The generation born with them, nor seemed
Less aged than the hoary trees and rocks
Around them;—and there have been holy men
Who deemed it were not well to pass life thus.
But let me often to these solitudes
Retire, and in thy presence reassure
My feeble virtue. Here its enemies,
The passions, at thy plainer footsteps shrink
And tremble and are still. O God! when thou
Dost scare the world with tempests, set on fire
The heavens with falling thunderbolts, or fill,
With all the waters of the firmament,
The swift dark whirlwind that uproots the woods
And drowns the villages; when, at thy call,
Uprises the great deep and throws himself
Upon the continent, and overwhelms
Its cities—who forgets not, at the sight

Of these tremendous tokens of thy power,
His pride, and lays his strifes and follies by?
Oh, from these sterner aspects of thy face
Spare me and mine, nor let us need the wrath
Of the mad, unchained elements to teach
Who rules them. Be it ours to meditate,
In these calm shades, thy milder majesty,
And to the beautiful order of thy works
Learn to conform the order of our lives.

June

I gazed upon the glorious sky
   And the green mountains round,
And thought that when I came to lie
   At rest within the ground,
'Twere pleasant, that in flowery June,
When brooks send up a cheerful tune,
   And groves a joyous sound,
The sexton's hand, my grave to make,
The rich, green mountain-turf should break.

A cell within the frozen mould,
   A coffin borne through sleet,
And icy clods above it rolled,
   While fierce the tempests beat—
Away! —I will not think of these—
Blue be the sky and soft the breeze,
   Earth green beneath the feet,
And be the damp mould gently pressed
Into my narrow place of rest.

There through the long, long summer hours,
   The golden light should lie,
And thick young herbs and groups of flowers
   Stand in their beauty by.
The oriole should build and tell
His love-tale close beside my cell;
   The idle butterfly
Should rest him there, and there be heard
The housewife bee and humming-bird.

And what if cheerful shouts at noon
   Come, from the village sent,
Or song of maids, beneath the moon
   With fairy laughter blent?
And what if, in the evening light,
Betrothed lovers walk in sight
   Of my low monument?
I would the lovely scene around
Might know no sadder sight nor sound.

I know that I no more should see
    The season's glorious show,
Nor would its brightness shine for me,
    Nor its wild music flow;
But if, around my place of sleep,
The friends I love should come to weep,
    They might not haste to go.
Soft airs, and song, and light, and bloom
Should keep them lingering by my tomb.

These to their softened hearts should bear
    The thought of what has been,
And speak of one who cannot share
    The gladness of the scene;
Whose part, in all the pomp that fills
The circuit of the summer hills,
    Is that his grave is green;
And deeply would their hearts rejoice
To hear again his living voice.

To the Fringed Gentian

Thou blossom bright with autumn dew,
And colored with the heaven's own blue,
That openest when the quiet light
Succeeds the keen and frosty night.

Thou comest not when violets lean
O'er wandering brooks and springs unseen,
Or columbines, in purple dressed,
Nod o'er the ground-bird's hidden nest.

Thou waitest late and com'st alone,
When woods are bare and birds are flown,
And frosts and shortening days portend
The aged year is near his end.

Then doth thy sweet and quiet eye
Look through its fringes to the sky,
Blue–blue–as if that sky let fall
A flower from its cerulean wall.

I would that thus, when I shall see
The hour of death draw near to me,
Hope, blossoming within my heart,
May look to heaven as I depart.

November

Yet one smile more, departing, distant sun!
　　One mellow smile through the soft vapory air,
Ere, o'er the frozen earth, the loud winds run,
　　Or snows are sifted o'er the meadows bare.
One smile on the brown hills and naked trees,
　　And the dark rocks whose summer wreaths are cast,
And the blue gentian-flower, that, in the breeze,
　　Nods lonely, of her beauteous race the last.
Yet a few sunny days, in which the bee
　　Shall murmur by the hedge that skirts the way,
The cricket chirp upon the russet lea,
　　And man delight to linger in thy ray.
Yet one rich smile, and we will try to bear
The piercing winter frost, and winds, and darkened air.

The Two Graves

'Tis a bleak wild hill, but green and bright
In the summer warmth and the mid-day light;
There's the hum of the bee and the chirp of the wren
And the dash of the brook from the alder-glen.
There's the sound of a bell from the scattered flock,
And the shade of the beech lies cool on the rock,
And fresh from the west is the free wind's breath—
There is nothing here that speaks of death.

Far yonder, where orchards and gardens lie,
And dwellings cluster, 'tis there men die,
They are born, they die, and are buried near,
Where the populous graveyard lightens the bier.
For strict and close are the ties that bind
In death the children of human-kind;
Yea, stricter and closer than those of life,—
'Tis a neighborhood that knows no strife.
They are noiselessly gathered—friend and foe—
To the still and dark assemblies below.
Without a frown or a smile they meet,
Each pale and calm in his winding-sheet;
In that sullen home of peace and gloom,
Crowded, like guests in a banquet-room.

Yet there are graves in this lonely spot,
Two humble graves,—but I meet them not.
I have seen them,—eighteen years are past
Since I found their place in the brambles last,—
The place where, fifty winters ago,
An aged man in his locks of snow,
And an aged matron, withered with years,
Were solemnly laid!—but not with tears.
For none, who sat by the light of their hearth,
Beheld their coffins covered with earth;
Their kindred were far, and their children dead,
When the funeral-prayer was coldly said.

Two low green hillocks, two small gray stones,
Rose over the place that held their bones;

But the grassy hillocks are levelled again,
And the keenest eye might search in vain,
'Mong briers, and ferns, and paths of sheep,
For the spot where the aged couple sleep.

Yet well might they lay, beneath the soil
Of this lonely spot, that man of toil,
And trench the strong hard mould with the spade,
Where never before a grave was made;
For he hewed the dark old woods away,
And gave the virgin fields to the day;
And the gourd and the bean, beside, his door,
Bloomed where their flowers ne'er opened before;
And the maize stood up, and the bearded rye
Bent low in the breath of an unknown sky.

'Tis said that when life is ended here,
The spirit is borne to a distant sphere;
That it visits its earthly home no more,
Nor looks on the haunts it loved before.
But why should the bodiless soul be sent
Far off, to a long, long banishment?
Talk not of the light and the living green!
It will pine for the dear familiar scene;
It will yearn, in that strange bright world, to behold
The rock and the stream it knew of old.

'Tis a cruel creed, believe it not!
Death to the good is a milder lot.
They are here,–they are here,–that harmless pair,
In the yellow sunshine and flowing air,
In the light cloud-shadows that slowly pass,
In the sounds that rise from the murmuring grass.
They sit where their humble cottage stood,
They walk by the waving edge of the wood,
And list to the long-accustomed flow
Of the brook that wets the rocks below,
Patient, and peaceful, and passionless,
As seasons on seasons swiftly press,
They watch, and wait, and linger around,
Till the day when their bodies shall leave the ground.

The Prairies

These are the gardens of the Desert, these
The unshorn fields, boundless and beautiful,
For which the speech of England has no name–
The Prairies. I behold them for the first,
And my heart swells, while the dilated sight
Takes in the encircling vastness. Lo! they stretch,
In airy undulations, far away,
As if the ocean, in his gentlest swell,
Stood still, with all his rounded billows fixed,
And motionless forever. –Motionless? –
No–they are all unchained again. The clouds
Sweep over with their shadows, and, beneath,
The surface rolls and fluctuates to the eye;
Dark hollows seem to glide along and chase
The sunny ridges. Breezes of the South!
Who toss the golden and the flame-like flowers,
And pass the prairie-hawk that, poised on high,
Flaps his broad wings, yet moves not–ye have played
Among the palms of Mexico and vines
Of Texas, and have crisped the limpid brooks
That from the fountains of Sonora glide
Into the calm Pacific–have ye fanned
A nobler or a lovelier scene than this?
Man hath no power in all this glorious work:
The hand that built the firmament hath heaved
And smoothed these verdant swells, and sown their slopes
With herbage, planted them with island groves,
And hedged them round with forests. Fitting floor
For this magnificent temple of the sky–
With flowers whose glory and whose multitude
Rival the constellations! The great heavens
Seem to stoop down upon the scene in love,–
A nearer vault, and of a tenderer blue,
Than that which bends above our eastern hills.

As o'er the verdant waste I guide my steed,
Among the high rank grass that sweeps his sides

The hollow beating of his footstep seems
A sacrilegious sound. I think of those
Upon whose rest he tramples. Are they here–
The dead of other days?–and did the dust
Of these fair solitudes once stir with life
And burn with passion? Let the mighty mounds
That overlook the rivers, or that rise
In the dim forest crowded with old oaks,
Answer. A race, that long has passed away,
Built them;–a disciplined and populous race
Heaped, with long toil, the earth, while yet the Greek
Was hewing the Pentelicus to forms
Of symmetry, and rearing on its rock
The glittering Parthenon. These ample fields
Nourished their harvests, here their herds were fed,
When haply by their stalls the bison lowed,
And bowed his maned shoulder to the yoke.
All day this desert murmured with their toils,
Till twilight blushed, and lovers walked, and wooed
In a forgotten language, and old tunes,
From instruments of unremembered form,
Gave the soft winds a voice. The red man came–
The roaming hunter tribes, warlike and fierce,
And the mound-builders vanished from the earth.
The solitude of centuries untold
Has settled where they dwelt. The prairie-wolf
Hunts in their meadows, and his fresh-dug den
Yawns by my path. The gopher mines the ground
Where stood their swarming cities. All is gone;
All–save the piles of earth that hold their bones,
The platforms where they worshipped unknown gods,
The barriers which they builded from the soil
To keep the foe at bay–till o'er the walls
The wild beleaguerers broke, and, one by one,
The strongholds of the plain were forced, and heaped
With corpses. The brown vultures of the wood
Flocked to those vast uncovered sepulchres,
And sat unscared and silent at their feast.

Haply some solitary fugitive,
Lurking in marsh and forest, till the sense
Of desolation and of fear became
Bitterer than death, yielded himself to die.
Man's better nature triumphed then. Kind words
Welcomed and soothed him; the rude conquerors
Seated the captive with their chiefs; he chose
A bride among their maidens, and at length
Seemed to forget–yet ne'er forgot–the wife
Of his first love, and her sweet little ones,
Butchered, amid their shrieks, with all his race.

   Thus change the forms of being. Thus arise
Races of living things, glorious in strength,
And perish, as the quickening breath of God
Fills them, or is withdrawn. The red man, too,
Has left the blooming wilds he ranged so long,
And, nearer to the Rocky Mountains, sought
A wilder hunting-ground. The beaver builds
No longer by these streams, but far away,
On waters whose blue surface ne'er gave back
The white man's face–among Missouri's springs,
And pools whose issues swell the Oregon–
He rears his little Venice. In these plains
The bison feeds no more. Twice twenty leagues
Beyond remotest smoke of hunter's camp,
Roams the majestic brute, in herds that shake
The earth with thundering steps–yet here I meet
His ancient footprints stamped beside the pool.

   Still this great solitude is quick with life.
Myriads of insects, gaudy as the flowers
They flutter over, gentle quadrupeds,
And birds, that scarce have learned the fear of man,
Are here, and sliding reptiles of the ground,
Startlingly beautiful. The graceful deer
Bounds to the wood at my approach. The bee,
A more adventurous colonist than man,
With whom he came across the eastern deep,

Fills the savannas with his murmurings,
And hides his sweets, as in the golden age,
Within the hollow oak. I listen long
To his domestic hum, and think I hear
The sound of that advancing multitude
Which soon shall fill these deserts. From the ground
Comes up the laugh of children, the soft voice
Of maidens, and the sweet and solemn hymn
Of Sabbath worshippers. The low of herds
Blends with the rustling of the heavy grain
Over the dark brown furrows. All at once
A fresher wind sweeps by, and breaks my dream,
And I am in the wilderness alone.

The Knight's Epitaph

This is the church which Pisa, great and free,
Reared to St. Catharine. How the time-stained walls,
That earthquakes shook not from their poise, appear
To shiver in the deep and voluble tones
Rolled from the organ! Underneath my feet
There lies the lid of a sepulchral vault.
The image of an armed knight is graven
Upon it, clad in perfect panoply–
Cuishes, and greaves, and cuirass, with barred helm,
Gauntleted hand, and sword, and blazoned shield.
Around, in Gothic characters, worn dim
By feet of worshippers, are traced his name,
And birth, and death, and words of eulogy.
Why should I pore upon them? This old tomb,
This effigy, the strange disused form
Of this inscription, eloquently show
His history. Let me clothe in fitting words
The thoughts they breathe, and frame his epitaph:

"He whose forgotten dust for centuries
Has lain beneath this stone, was one in whom
Adventure, and endurance, and emprise,
Exalted the mind's faculties and strung
The body's sinews. Brave he was in fight,
Courteous in banquet, scornful of repose,
And bountiful, and cruel, and devout,
And quick to draw the sword in private feud,
He pushed his quarrels to the death, yet prayed
The saints as fervently on bended knees
As ever shaven cenobite. He loved
As fiercely as he fought. He would have borne
The maid that pleased him from her bower by night
To his hill castle, as the eagle bears
His victim from the fold, and rolled the rocks
On his pursuers. He aspired to see
His native Pisa queen and arbitress
Of cities; earnestly for her he raised

His voice in council, and affronted death
In battle-field, and climbed the galley's deck,
And brought the captured flag of Genoa back,
Or piled upon the Arno's crowded quay
The glittering spoils of the tamed Saracen.
He was not born to brook the stranger's yoke,
But would have joined the exiles that withdrew
Forever, when the Florentine broke in
The gates of Pisa, and bore off the bolts
For trophies—but he died before that day.

   "He lived, the impersonation of an age
That never shall return. His soul of fire
Was kindled by the breath of the rude time
He lived in. Now a gentler race succeeds,
Shuddering at blood; the effeminate cavalier,
Turning his eyes from the reproachful past,
And from the hopeless future, gives to ease,
And love, and music, his inglorious life."

The Living Lost

Matron! the children of whose love,
   Each to his grave, in youth have passed;
And now the mould is heaped above
   The dearest and the last!
Bride! who dost wear the widow's veil
Before the wedding flowers are pale!
Ye deem the human heart endures
No deeper, bitterer grief than yours.

Yet there are pangs of keener woe,
   Of which the sufferers never speak,
Nor to the world's cold pity show
   The tears that scald the cheek,
Wrung from their eyelids by the shame
And guilt of those they shrink to name,
Whom once they loved with cheerful will,
And love, though fallen and branded, still.

Weep, ye who sorrow for the dead,
   Thus breaking hearts their pain relieve,
And reverenced are the tears they shed,
   And honored ye who grieve.
The praise of those who sleep in earth,
The pleasant memory of their worth,
The hope to meet when life is past,
Shall heal the tortured mind at last.

But ye, who for the living lost
   That agony in secret bear,
Who shall with soothing words accost
   The strength of your despair?
Grief for your sake is scorn for them
Whom ye lament and all condemn;
And o'er the world of spirits lies
A gloom from which ye turn your eyes.

The Old Man's Counsel

Among our hills and valleys, I have known
Wise and grave men, who, while their diligent hands
Tended or gathered in the fruits of earth,
Were reverent learners in the solemn school
Of Nature. Not in vain to them were sent
Seed-time and harvest, or the vernal shower
That darkened the brown tilth, or snow that beat
On the white winter hills. Each brought, in turn,
Some truth, some lesson on the life of man,
Or recognition of the Eternal mind
Who veils his glory with the elements.

One such I knew long since, a white-haired man,
Pithy of speech, and merry when he would;
A genial optimist, who daily drew
From what he saw his quaint moralities.
Kindly he held communion, though so old,
With me a dreaming boy, and taught me much
That books tell not, and I shall ne'er forget.

The sun of May was bright in middle heaven,
And steeped the sprouting forests, the green hills,
And emerald wheat-fields, in his yellow light.
Upon the apple-tree, where rosy buds
Stood clustered, ready to burst forth in bloom,
The robin warbled forth his full clear note
For hours, and wearied not. Within the woods,
Whose young and half transparent leaves scarce cast
A shade, gay circles of anemones
Danced on their stalks; the shad-bush, white with flowers,
Brightened the glens; the new-leaved butternut
And quivering poplar to the roving breeze
Gave a balsamic fragrance. In the fields
I saw the pulses of the gentle wind
On the young grass. My heart was touched with joy
At so much beauty, flushing every hour
Into a fuller beauty; but my friend,

The thoughtful ancient, standing at my side,
Gazed on it mildly sad. I asked him why.

   "Well mayst thou join in gladness," he replied,
"With the glad earth, her springing plants and flowers,
And this soft wind, the herald of the green
Luxuriant summer. Thou art young like them,
And well mayst thou rejoice. But while the flight
Of seasons fills and knits thy spreading frame,
It withers mine, and thins my hair, and dims
These eyes, whose fading light shall soon be quenched
In utter darkness. Hearest thou that bird?"

   I listened, and from midst the depth of woods
Heard the love-signal of the grouse, that wears
A sable ruff around his mottled neck;
Partridge they call him by our northern streams,
And pheasant by the Delaware. He beat
His barred sides with his speckled wings, and made
A sound like distant thunder; slow the strokes
At first, then fast and faster, till at length
They passed into a murmur and were still.

   "There hast thou," said my friend, "a fitting type
Of human life. 'Tis an old truth, I know,
But images like these revive the power
Of long familiar truths. Slow pass our days
In childhood, and the hours of light are long
Betwixt the morn and eve; with swifter lapse
They glide in manhood, and in age they fly;
Till days and seasons flit before the mind
As flit the snow-flakes in a winter storm,
Seen rather than distinguished. Ah! I seem
As if I sat within a helpless bark,
By swiftly-running waters hurried on
To shoot some mighty cliff. Along the banks
Grove after grove, rock after frowning rock,
Bare sands and pleasant homes, and flowery nooks,
And isles and whirlpools in the stream, appear
Each after each, but the devoted skiff

Darts by so swiftly that their images
Dwell not upon the mind, or only dwell
In dim confusion; faster yet I sweep
By other banks, and the great gulf is near.

"Wisely, my son, while yet thy days are long,
And this fair change of seasons passes slow,
Gather and treasure up the good they yield—
All that they teach of virtue, of pure thoughts
And kind affections, reverence for thy God
And for thy brethren; so when thou shalt come
Into these barren years, thou mayst not bring
A mind unfurnished and a withered heart."

Long since that white-haired ancient slept—but still,
When the red flower-buds crowd the orchard-bough,
And the ruffed grouse is drumming far within
The woods, his venerable form again
Is at my side, his voice is in my ear.

An Evening Revery

The summer day is closed—the sun is set:
Well they have done their office, those bright hours,
The latest of whose train goes softly out
In the red west. The green blade of the ground
Has risen, and herds have cropped it; the young twig
Has spread its plaited tissues to the sun;
Flowers of the garden and the waste have blown
And withered; seeds have fallen upon the soil,
From bursting cells, and in their graves await
Their resurrection. Insects from the pools
Have filled the air awhile with humming wings,
That now are still forever; painted moths
Have wandered the blue sky, and died again;
The mother-bird hath broken for her brood
Their prison shell, or shoved them from the nest,
Plumed for their earliest flight. In bright alcoves,
In woodland cottages with barky walls,
In noisome cells of the tumultuous town,
Mothers have clasped with joy the new-born babe.
Graves by the lonely forest, by the shore
Of rivers and of ocean, by the ways
Of the thronged city, have been hollowed out
And filled, and closed. This day hath parted friends
That ne'er before were parted; it hath knit
New friendships; it hath seen the maiden plight
Her faith, and trust her peace to him who long
Had wooed; and it hath heard, from lips which late
Were eloquent of love, the first harsh word,
That told the wedded one her peace was flown.

Farewell to the sweet sunshine! One glad day
Is added now to Childhood's merry days,
And one calm day to those of quiet Age.
Still the fleet hours run on; and as I lean,
Amid the thickening darkness, lamps are lit,

By those who watch the dead, and those who twine
Flowers for the bride. The mother from the eyes
Of her sick infant shades the painful light,
And sadly listens to the quick-drawn breath.

O thou great Movement of the Universe,
Or Change, or Flight of Time—for ye are one!
That bearest, silently, this visible scene
Into night's shadow and the streaming rays
Of starlight, whither art thou bearing me?
I feel the mighty current sweep me on,
Yet know not whither. Man foretells afar
The courses of the stars; the very hour
He knows when they shall darken or grow bright;
Yet doth the eclipse of Sorrow and of Death
Come unforwarned. Who next, of those I love,
Shall pass from life, or, sadder yet, shall fall
From virtue? Strife with foes, or bitterer strife
With friends, or shame and general scorn of men—
Which who can bear? – or the fierce rack of pain–
Lie they within my path? Or shall the years
Push me, with soft and inoffensive pace,
Into the stilly twilight of my age?
Or do the portals of another life
Even now, while I am glorying in my strength.
Impend around me? Oh! Beyond that bourne,
In the vast cycle of being which begins
At that dread threshold, with what fairer forms
Shall the great law of change and progress clothe
Its workings? Gently–so have good men taught–
Gently, and without grief, the old shall glide
Into the new; the eternal flow of things,
Like a bright river of the fields of heaven
Shall journey onward in perpetual peace.

The Snow-Shower

Stand here by my side and turn, I pray,
  On the lake below, thy gentle eyes;
The clouds hang over it, heavy and gray,
  And dark and silent the water lies;
And out of that frozen mist the snow
In wavering flakes begins to flow;
          Flake after flake
They sink in the dark and silent lake.

See how in a living swarm they come
  From the chambers beyond that misty veil;
Some hover awhile in air, and some
  Rush prone from the sky like summer hail.
All, dropping swiftly or settling slow,
Meet, and are still in the depths below;
          Flake after flake
Dissolved in the dark and silent lake.

Here delicate snow-stars, out of the cloud,
  Come floating downward in airy play,
Like spangles dropped from the glistening crowd
  That whiten by night the milky way;
There broader and burlier masses fall;
The sullen water buries them all—
          Flake after flake—
All drowned in the dark and silent lake.

And some, as on tender wings they glide
  From their chilly birth-cloud, dim and gray,
Are joined in their fall, and, side by side,
  Come clinging along their unsteady way;
As friend with friend, or husband with wife,
Makes hand in hand the passage of life;
          Each mated flake
Soon sinks in the dark and silent lake.

Lo! while we are gazing, in swifter haste
   Stream down the snows, till the air is white,
As, myriads by myriads madly chased,
They fling themselves from their shadowy height.
   The fair, frail creatures of middle sky,
What speed they make, with their grave so nigh;
         Flake after flake,
To lie in the dark and silent lake!

I see in thy gentle eyes a tear;
   They turn to me in sorrowful thought;
Thou thinkest of friends, the good and dear,
   Who were for a time, and now are not;
Like these fair children of cloud and frost,
That glisten a moment and then are lost,
         Flake after flake–
All lost in the dark and silent lake.

Yet look again, for the clouds divide;
   A gleam of blue on the water lies;
And far away, on the mountain-side,
   A sunbeam falls from the opening skies,
But the hurrying host that flew between
The cloud and the water, no more is seen;
         Flake after flake,
At rest in the dark and silent lake.

"Earth's Children Cleave to Earth"

Earth's children cleave to Earth–her frail
Decaying children dread decay.
Yon wreath of mist that leaves the vale
And lessens in the morning ray–
Look, how, by mountain rivulet,
It lingers as it upward creeps,
And clings to fern and copsewood set
Along the green and dewy steeps:
Clings to the flowery kalmia, clings
To precipices fringed with grass,
Dark maples where the wood-thrush sings,
And bowers of fragrant sassafras.
Yet all in vain–it passes still
From hold to hold, it cannot stay,
And in the very beams that fill
The world with glory, wastes away,
Till, parting from the mountain's brow,
It vanishes from human eye,
And that which sprung of earth is now
Assumed into the glorious sky.

The Planting of the Apple-Tree

Come, let us plant the apple-tree.
Cleave the tough greensward with the spade;
Wide let its hollow bed be made;
There gently lay the roots, and there
Sift the dark mould with kindly care,
    And press it o'er them tenderly,
As, round the sleeping infant's feet,
We softly fold the cradle-sheet;
    So plant we the apple-tree.

What plant we in this apple-tree?
Buds, which the breath of summer days
Shall lengthen into leafy sprays;
Boughs where the thrush, with crimson breast,
Shall haunt and sing and hide her nest;
    We plant, upon the sunny lea,
A shadow for the noontide hour,
A shelter from the summer shower,
    When we plant the apple-tree.

What plant we in this apple-tree?
Sweets for a hundred flowery springs
To load the May-wind's restless wings,
When, from the orchard-row, he pours
Its fragrance through our open doors;
    A world of blossoms for the bee,
Flowers for the sick girl's silent room,
For the glad infant sprigs of bloom,
    We plant with the apple-tree.

What plant we in this apple-tree?
Fruits that shall swell in sunny June,
And redden in the August noon,
And drop, when gentle airs come by,
That fan the blue September sky,
    While children come, with cries of glee,
And seek them where the fragrant grass
Betrays their bed to those who pass,

At the foot of the apple-tree.
And when, above this apple-tree,
The winter stars are quivering bright,
And winds go howling through the night,
Girls, whose young eyes o'erflow with mirth,
Shall peel its fruit by cottage-hearth,

And guests in prouder homes shall see,
Heaped with the grape of Cintra's vine
And golden orange of the line,
The fruit of the apple-tree

The fruitage of this apple-tree
Winds and our flag of stripe and star
Shall bear to coasts that lie afar,
Where men shall wonder at the view,
And ask in what fair groves they grew;

And sojourners beyond the sea
Shall think of childhood's careless day,
And long, long hours of summer play,
In the shade of the apple-tree.

Each year shall give this apple-tree
A broader flush of roseate bloom,
A deeper maze of verdurous gloom,
And loosen, when the frost-clouds lower,
The crisp brown leaves in thicker shower.

The years shall come and pass, but we
Shall hear no longer, where we lie,
The summer's songs, the autumn's sigh,
In the boughs of the apple-tree.

And time shall waste this apple-tree.
Oh, when its aged branches throw
Thin shadows on the ground below,
Shall fraud and force and iron will
Oppress the weak and helpless still?

What shall the tasks of mercy be,
Amid the toils, the strifes, the tears
Of those who live when length of years
Is wasting this little apple-tree?

"Who planted this old apple-tree?"
The children of that distant day
Thus to some aged man shall say;
And, gazing on its mossy stem,
The gray-haired man shall answer them:
  "A poet of the land was he,
Born in the rude but good old times;
'Tis said he made some quaint old rhymes,
  On planting the apple-tree."

The Third of November, 1861

Softly breathes the west-wind beside the ruddy forest,
  Taking leaf by leaf from the branches where he flies.
Sweetly streams the sunshine, this third day of November,
  Through the golden haze of the quiet autumn skies.

Tenderly the season has spared the grassy meadows,
  Spared the petted flowers that the old world gave the new,
Spared the autumn-rose and the garden's group of pansies,
  Late-blown dandelions and periwinkles blue.

On my cornice linger the ripe black grapes ungathered;
  Children fill the groves with the echoes of their glee,
Gathering tawny chestnuts, and shouting when beside them
  Drops the heavy fruit of the tall black-walnut tree.

Glorious are the woods in their latest gold and crimson,
  Yet our full-leaved willows are in their freshest green.
Such a kindly autumn, so mercifully dealing
  With the growths of summer, I never yet have seen.

Like this kindly season may life's decline come o'er me;
  Past is manhood's summer, the frosty months are here;
Yet be genial airs and a pleasant sunshine left me,
  Leaf, and fruit, and blossom, to mark the closing year!

Dreary is the time when the flowers of earth are withered;
  Dreary is the time when the woodland leaves are cast—
When, upon the hillside, all hardened into iron,
  Howling, like a wolf, flies the famished northern blast.

Dreary are the years when the eye can look no longer
  With delight on Nature, or hope on human kind;
Oh, may those that whiten my temples, as they pass me,
  Leave the heart unfrozen, and spare the cheerful mind!

The Poet

Thou, who wouldst wear the name
  Of poet mid thy brethren of mankind,
And clothe in words of flame
  Thoughts that shall live within the general mind!
Deem not the framing of a deathless lay
The pastime of a drowsy summer day.

But gather all thy powers,
  And wreak them on the verse that thou dost weave,
And in thy lonely hours,
  At silent morning or at wakeful eve,
While the warm current tingles through thy veins,
Set forth the burning words in fluent strains.

No smooth array of phrase,
  Artfully sought and ordered though it be,
Which the cold rhymer lays
  Upon his page with languid industry,
Can wake the listless pulse to livelier speed,
Or fill with sudden tears the eyes that read.

The secret wouldst thou know
  To touch the heart or fire the blood at will?
Let thine own eyes o'erflow;
  Let thy lips quiver with the passionate thrill;
Seize the great thought, ere yet its power be past,
And bind, in words, the fleet emotion fast.

Then, should thy verse appear
  Halting and harsh, and all unaptly wrought,
Touch the crude line with fear,
  Save in the moment of impassioned thought;
Then summon back the original glow, and mend
The strain with rapture that with fire was penned.

Yet let no empty gust
  Of passion find an utterance in thy lay,
A blast that whirls the dust
  Along the howling street and dies away;

But feelings of calm power and mighty sweep,
Like currents journeying through the windless deep.

Seek'st thou, in living lays,
    To limn the beauty of the earth and sky?
Before thine inner gaze
    Let all that beauty in clear vision lie;
Look on it with exceeding love, and write
The words inspired by wonder and delight.

Of tempests wouldst thou sing,
    Or tell of battle–make thyself a part
Of the great tumult; cling
    To the tossed wreck with terror in thy heart;
Scale, with the assaulting host, the rampart's height,
 And strike and struggle in the thickest fight.

So shalt thou frame a lay
    That haply may endure from age to age,
And they who read shall say:
    "What witchery hangs upon this poet's page!
What art is his the written spells to find
That sway from mood to mood the willing mind!"

The Path

The path we planned beneath October's sky,
   Along the hillside, through the woodland shade,
Is finished; thanks to thee, whose kindly eye
   Has watched me, as I plied the busy spade;
Else had I wearied, ere this path of ours
Had pierced the woodland to its inner bowers.

Yet, 'twas a pleasant toil to trace and beat,
   Among the glowing trees, this winding way,
While the sweet autumn sunshine, doubly sweet,
   Flushed with the ruddy foliage, round us lay,
As if some gorgeous cloud of morning stood,
In glory, mid the arches of the wood.

A path! what beauty does a path bestow
   Even on the dreariest wild! its savage nooks
Seem homelike where accustomed footsteps go,
   And the grim rock puts on familiar looks.
The tangled swamp, through which a pathway strays,
Becomes a garden with strange flowers and sprays.

See from the weedy earth a rivulet break
   And purl along the untrodden wilderness;
There the shy cuckoo comes his thirst to slake,
   There the shrill jay alights his plumes to dress;
And there the stealthy fox, when morn is gray,
Laps the clear stream and lightly moves away.

But let a path approach that fountain's brink,
   And nobler forms of life, behold! are there:
Boys kneeling with protruded lips to drink,
   And slender maids that homeward slowly bear
The brimming pail, and busy dames that lay
Their webs to whiten in the summer ray.

Then know we that for herd and flock are poured
   Those pleasant streams that o'er the pebbles slip;
Those pure sweet waters sparkle on the board;
   Those fresh cool waters wet the sick man's lip;
Those clear bright waters from the font are shed,

In dews of baptism, on the infant's head.
What different steps the rural footway trace!
   The laborer afield at early day;
The schoolboy sauntering with uneven pace;
   The Sunday worshipper in fresh array;
And mourner in the weeds of sorrow drest,
And, smiling to himself, the wedding guest.

There he who cons a speech and he who hums
   His yet unfinished verses, musing walk.
There, with her little brood, the matron comes,
   To break the spring flower from its juicy stalk;
And lovers, loitering, wonder that the moon
Has risen upon their pleasant stroll so soon.

Bewildered in vast woods, the traveller feels
   His heavy heart grow lighter, if he meet
The traces of a path, and straight he kneels,
   And kisses the dear print of human feet,
And thanks his God, and journeys without fear,
For now he knows the abodes of men are near.

Pursue the slenderest path across a lawn:
   Lo! on the broad highway it issues forth,
And, blended with the greater track, goes on,
   Over the surface of the mighty earth,
Climbs hills and crosses vales, and stretches far,
   Through silent forests, toward the evening star—

And enters cities murmuring with the feet
   Of multitudes, and wanders forth again,
And joins the chimes of frost to climes of heat,
   Binds East to West, and marries main to main,
Nor stays till at the long-resounding shore
Of the great deep, where paths are known no more.

Oh, mighty instinct, that dost thus unite
   Earth's neighborhoods and tribes with friendly bands,
What guilt is theirs who, in their greed or spite,
   Undo thy holy work with violent hands,
And post their squadrons, nursed in war's grim trade,
To bar the ways for mutual succor made!

Two

Tales

A Pennsylvania Legend

Is the world to become altogether philosophical and rational? Are we to believe nothing that we cannot account for from natural causes? Are tales of supernatural warnings, of the interposition and visible appearance of disembodied spirits, to be laughed out of countenance and forgotten? There are people who have found out that to imagine any other modes of being than those of which our experience tells us, is extremely ridiculous. Alas! we shall soon learn to believe that the material world is the only world, and that the things which are the objects of our external senses are the only things which have an existence. Recollect, gentlemen, that you may carry your philosophy too far. You forget how the human mind delights in superstition. You are welcome to explode such of its delusions as are hurtful, but leave us, I pray you, a few of such as are harmless; leave us, at least, those which are interesting to our hearts, without making us forget our love and duty to our fellow creatures.

As long, however, as there are aged crones to talk, and children to listen, the labours of philosophy cannot be crowned with perfect success. A dread of supernatural visitations, awakened in our tender years, keeps possession of the mind like an instinct, and bids defiance to the attempts of reason to dislodge it. For my part, I look upon myself as a debtor to the old nurses and servant maids, who kept me from my sleep with tales of goblins and apparitions, for one of the highest pleasures I enjoy. It is owing to them, I believe, that I read, with a deep sense of delight, narratives which seem to inspire many of my enlightened and reasoning acquaintances with no feelings but that of disgust. Yet I cannot but notice a remarkable scarcity of well-attested incidents of this sort in modern years. The incredulity of the age has caused the supernatural interpositions, that were once so frequent, to be withdrawn; portents and prodigies are not shown to mockers, and spectres will not walk abroad to be made the subjects of philosophical analysis. Yet some parts of our country are more favoured in this respect than others. The old beldames among the German settlers of Pennsylvania tell in the greedy ears of their children the marvellous legends of the country from which they had their origin, and to the deep awe and undoubting reverence with which these are related and received, it is probably owing that the day of wonders is not past among that people. Let the European writer gather up the traditions of his country; I will employ a leisure moment in recording one of the fresher, but not less authentic, legends of ours.

Walter Buckel was a German emigrant, who came over to Pennsylvania about sixty years ago. He was of gentle blood, and used to boast of his relationship to one of the most illustrious houses in his native country. Nor was this an idle boast, for he could trace his pedigree with perfect accuracy through ten generations up to a hunch-backed baron, from whose clandestine amours with a milkmaid, sprung the founder of the family of the Buckels. The offspring of these stolen loves did not disgrace his birth, for he inherited all the pride and deformity of his father. So vain was he of his personal resemblance to his noble parent, that he assumed the surname of Buckel, from the hump on his shoulders, and transmitted the name and the hump to his posterity. The family continued to wear this badge of their descent down to the time of Walter Buckel; and it was observed that, whenever it waned from its due magnitude in one generation, it was sure to rise with added roundness and prominence in another. As, however, the illustrious extraction, of which it was the symbol, grew more remote, the respect with which the neighbours regarded it diminished, and finally ceased altogether.

Walter Buckel, determined to form no connexion unworthy of his birth, had married one of his cousins, a fair, fat, flaxen-haired maiden, the purity of whose blood was attested by a hump like his own. Walter was one of those unfortunate men who are perpetually looking for respect, and perpetually disappointed, by meeting with nothing but ridicule: he had hoped to increase his consideration among his acquaintances by this marriage; but their jeers came faster and coarser, and so many rustic jokes were cracked on the well-matched couple, that he almost grew weary of life. In his desperation, he sold the patrimonial estate on which he subsisted, and without bidding adieu to any of his neighbours except the curate, who used sometimes, induced by his benevolence, to come and talk to him about the antiquity and dignity of his family, and carry home a pig, or a turkey, or a shoulder of mutton, he emigrated to America, and settled down upon four hundred acres of wild land, in the interior of the state of Pennsylvania.

His first care was to provide a shelter for his family. His new neighbours, most of whom were recent settlers like himself, came together the morning after his arrival, and before the sun had gone down, a comfortable log house, with two rooms, was ready for their reception. It was built at the foot of a small hill, in a little natural opening of the forest, under a fine flourishing tree, of that species commonly called the red oak, which, in favourable soils, and in the open country, grows to a great size, and with a most beautiful symmetry, its long lusty boughs given off in whorls at regular distances, and its smooth bark of a greenish-brown colour, looking as if ready to burst with the luxuriance of its juices. The tree was one of the finest of its kind, and stood in the centre of a circle of rich turf, about half an acre in extent, the circumference of which was fenced by a natural hedge of under-growth, that prevented you from looking into the darkness and solitude of the surrounding woods. A brook came down the hill, and ran noisily through the cheerful spot, over the round stones, among which were seen a few straggling roots of the oak, laid bare by the action of the current.

Walter, who was a thin, bilious, bustling man, went to work in the bitterness and vexation of his heart, thinking sometimes of his genealogy, sometimes of the gibes and jeers of acquaintances, and sometimes of his voluntary exile from his native country, until he had cleared the wood from all that part of the farm which lay south of the house, and was judged to include about one third of the whole. The rest he suffered to lie in its wild state, for the purpose of supplying with fuel the fire that roared all winter in the enormous chimney, which occupied a full half of the room called the kitchen. In the mean time, his wife was not idle; before the year came round she presented him with a son, whom he named Caspar, a name which, according to the family tradition, belonged to their ancestor, the hunch-backed baron.

It has been said, that marriages between relations not only perpetuate, but even aggravate, the physical and mental deformities of the parents in their offspring. I cannot tell if this be so; I was never willing to believe it; but whenever I think of the case of Caspar Buckel, I am staggered in my unbelief. As he grew to the age of puberty, it was remarked that he inherited the self-conccit and the uneasy temper of his father, along with the sullen taciturnity of his mother. The corpulency of the one seemed to have fixed itself in his back and belly, while the spare habit of the other was copied in his lean arms, his shrunk loins, and slender legs. The hump on his shoulders was at least two inches higher than that of either of his parents; his forehead was traversed by a thousand crossing wrinkles; his flabby cheeks were seamed with longitudinal furrows, and hung down so low on each side of his peaked chin, as to give him the appearance of having three chins at once. Two small dim gray eyes peeped from under two white shaggy brows; between them the nose seemed as if absorbed into the face, but re-appeared at a prodigious distance below; and above, a bushy shock of carroty hair stared in all directions.

At an early age, Caspar had an appearance of decrepitude; nobody who looked at him would have thought him younger than his father. Yet this singular being was not without his enjoyments. He had often heard his father speak of his noble extraction, and this idea became to him the occasion of great inward glorying, when he looked upon the earth-born plebeians around him. But it was a pleasure of a deeper and more thrilling nature, to listen to the marvellous stories doled out by a toothless old female domestic, whom his father brought with him from Germany, and who was now too old and infirm to do any thing but smoke her pipe, and tell old tales by the fire-side. She told him of fairies, who dwell by day in the chambers of the earth, and dance by night in solitary groves; of hairy wood-demons, and swart goblins of the mine, till his little eyes shone with a fixed glare, and his bushy hair looked as if it would disentangle and straighten itself with terror.

Caspar liked neither to work nor to go to school, and his parents were too kind to think of compelling him to do either; his boyish days were consequently passed under the great oak. He whiled away the still summer mornings in chucking pebbles into the brook; in the heat of the day he slept with the dog in the shade, or climbed up to a seat among the thick boughs and leaves, and built castles in the air; and when the cooler breezes sprung up in the afternoon, he amused himself with swinging in a long rope, the two ends of which he had tied to two strong neighbouring branches. But if the tree was thus necessary to his amusements, it was also the strengthener of his superstitions. His bed was in a kind of loft just under the eaves of the house; and in the stormy autumnal nights, as he lay thinking over the legends of the old female domestic, he heard with terror the distant roar of the wind wrestling with the trees of the forest. At length he heard it fall with fury upon the oak itself, and then a storm of big rain-drops would be shaken from its boughs, and a shower of acorns would rattle down; and the long branches would lash the roof, till it seemed to him as if all the fiends of the woodland had fastened upon the old log cabin, and were going to fly away with it.

Walter Buckel now found himself growing rich, and began to be ashamed of living in a log house at a distance from the highway, and under the shade of a great tree. He therefore imitated the example of some of his more prosperous neighbors and built a fine, huge, yellow house, about two hundred rods from his old dwelling, close to the public road, where there was not a bough to keep the summer heat from his door, where he might be continually stifled by the dust raised by loaded wagons and herds of cattle driven to the Philadelphia market, and where the passing traveller might look in at his windows; he then quitted his pleasant little nook, and demolished his log house. An American farmer, whether a native or an emigrant, cuts down a tree with as little ceremony as he cuts down ripe corn, and the oak would have shared the fate of the cabin it sheltered, had not Caspar, who intended to swing under its boughs many an idle afternoon yet, pleaded hard in its favour.

The toothless old female domestic, who had told Caspar so many goblin stories, survived this transplantation of the family but two months. At first Caspar cared very little about her death, but in a few days he felt severely the want of that excitement from her wild tales that had become habitual to him, and he began to feel a sincere grief for her loss. It became irksome to linger about his father's great new house; he grew sick of seeing carts, wagons, and cattle go by the door, and rambled away into the dark and still woods, like those in which the scene of most of the legends that had taken such strong hold of his mind were laid. He often remained out till the sun was down, and sometimes till the twilight was down also, and on his return expected at every step to be greeted by some gigantic mountain spirit, and peeped into many a dark thicket to see if it did not hide some dwarfish elf of the forest. To give Caspar his due, he did not seek these fearful interviews merely from a love of the wild and the terrible; his anticipations were all of good luck, and he considered the descendant of the hunch-backed German baron, as too important and too fortunate a personage to be regarded with any other feeling than good will by these powerful but capricious beings.

At length his father and mother died, both in the same year, and were decently laid in their graves. Caspar had then just come of age, and being left master of his father's estate, which was a very comfortable one, he was unwillingly forced into contact with the world. At first his neighbours, partly from natural civility, partly from a feeling of pity, and partly also, perhaps, from a respect to his wealth, were careful to suppress the mirth occasioned by his deformity, and his uncouth aspect and manners; but when they saw the undisguised contempt with which the misshapen creature treated them, they no longer kept any measures in their ridicule. The school boys chalked his figure on the board fences, the young men quizzed him, the girls ran away from him, and it was generally allowed by all who had any dealings with him, that it was a capital joke to cheat him.

All these things, however, moved him less than the scorn of the beautiful Adelaide Sippel, a German beauty, with an abundance of fair hair, a pair of roguish light blue eyes, and a neck and arms, none of the slenderest it is true, but of a milky whiteness. Caspar, after having fully considered the matter, had concluded to take a help-mate to assist him in the management of his estate, and had signified to Adelaide his intention of conferring the honour upon her, but she only laughed in his face. Soon afterwards he made a formal declaration of his passion, in a letter, the tenderest that the schoolmaster, under his special direction, could compose; but the only notice she deigned to take of it, was to send, by way of answer, an exact likeness of his own figure, carved out of a rickety mangel-wortzel. This rebuff almost stunned poor Caspar, who thenceforward resolved to have as little as possible to do with such an ill-judging and disrespectful world. He resumed his lonely rambles in the woods, and sought relief from his mortification by indulging the wild imaginations that formerly possessed him.

It was in a mild summer evening, when he had been out all day in the forest, and had thought more than usual of the scorn of Adelaide and the scoffs of the world, that he found himself under the great oak that once hung over his father's cabin. The twilight had just set in, and the frogs were piping in the marshes. "It is too early to go home yet," thought he, and he sat down on one of the logs of the old building, that lay half bedded in the earth, with wild flowers nodding over it, and began to mutter over the burden of his discontent. All at once he seemed to hear a sound as of a human voice, blended with a rustling of small boughs and leaves. He looked about him, but saw nothing. Again he heard the sound; it seemed to proceed from directly above his head. He looked up, and beheld high in the tree, and seemingly projecting from the side of the trunk next to him, a beautiful female voice, and a well-turned throat. The features were moulded in the finest symmetry–youthful–but with that look of youth which we see in Grecian statues, and may imagine to belong to beings whose lives are of a longer date than ours, and which seems as if never to pass away. On each side of the face flowed down a profusion of light brown hair, that played softly in the wind.

"Caspar, Caspar," said the voice.

"I am here," said Caspar, "what wouldst thou with me?"

"Art thou unhappy, Caspar?"

"Art thou a spirit, and askest that question," replied the youth; "dost thou not see my deformity, and dost thou not know that all the world laugh at me, and Adelaide slights me–and yet thou inquirest if I am unhappy."

"Caspar," returned the voice, "thou did once preserve my existence, and I have not forgotten the benefit. Wash thy hands and face in the little pool in that rivulet, and go thy way home, and thou wilt soon see that I am not ungrateful."

Caspar obeyed the direction, and returned home with a lightened heart. He went to bed, but could not sleep a wink for thinking of the adventure of the evening. When he rose in the morning, he fancied his hump was less heavy and unwieldy than the day before, and it is related that an old woman of the neighbourhood, who lived by herself in a little hut, and subsisted principally on charity, and who had come to his house to borrow, or rather beg, a bit of butter and a little tea, could not refrain from saying to him, "La! Mr. Buckel, how well you look this morning." Certain it is, however, that from that day there was a gradual and surprising change in his personal appearance. It seemed as if the superabundant bulk of his spider-like body was travelling into his shrunken arms and legs. The bridge of his nose rose from its humble level, and bent itself into a true Roman curve; his cheeks ascended to their proper place, his wrinkles went away one by one, his eyes filled and brightened, his brows darkened, and his chestnut hair curled the edge of a fine forehead. In a twelvemonth the transformation was complete. His shoulders had become straight, his limbs well-proportioned, and his waist, with a little reduction, would have satisfied any fashion-able coxcomb that struts Broadway in a corset. His height also had astonishingly increased. Formerly he wanted just an inch of five feet, and now he wanted but an inch of six. (I myself have seen the notch where he was measured, in one of the rooms of an old house then occupied as a tavern, and I carefully ascertained its distance from the floor by means of a three-foot rattan, which I commonly carry about with me.) Caspar had formerly a great aversion to looking-glasses, but now he consulted his mirror several times a day, and whenever he approached it, he could not help bowing to the graceful stranger whom he saw there.

Caspar's neighbours would not have recognised him after this change, had he not almost from the first forgotten his misanthropy in the delight it gave him. As soon as ever he became satisfied that it was real and progressive, he almost went mad with joy, and could not forbear hugging every body he met. The elderly ladies all declared that Mr. Buckel had a strange way with him, and the young ran shrieking from these vehement demonstrations of his good will. He mingled in the rustic sports of the young men at trainings, elections, and other holidays, and though a little awkward at first, he soon became a famous leaper and wrestler, and learned to throw a ball and pitch a quoit with as much dexterity as the best of them. Every body began to take a liking to a young man so handsome, good-humoured, and rich; the farmers who had daughters told him it was high time to think of getting married; the matrons expatiated in his presence on the good temper and industry of their girls; and, the buxom fair-haired German maidens never laughed so loud as when they thought him within hearing. Caspar, however, had not forgotten his first love; and when he again proposed himself in softer phrase to Adelaide Sippel, the blushes came over her fair temples and white neck, but she did not again reject him. They were married amid such fiddling and dancing, such piles of cakes and floods of whiskey, and such a tumult and tempest of rustic rejoicings, as had never before been known in the settlement.

A man of moderate fortune, who has not acquired habits of industry and attentive management of his estate, should content himself with living idly and easily; he cannot afford to live splendidly. Caspar was not aware of the truth of this maxim: he knew that he was richer than his neighbours; but he had never calculated what expenses he could incur without lessening his estate. He was resolved that his smiling wife should wear the finest clothes, and ride to church in the finest German wagon, drawn by the finest horses in the place. He loved society, the more, probably, for having been excluded from it in his youth; and sat long and late at the taverns with merry, jesting, catch-singing, roaring blades, from the old countries. He attended all the horse-races he could hear of, at which he betted deeply, and was taken in by the knowing ones. He was fond of hunting, and bought a rifle and a couple of hounds, and went into the woods in pursuit of game, day after day, during which the concerns of his farm took care of themselves. By such judicious methods he contrived to get himself pretty deeply in debt; he was dunned; he borrowed money of one man to pay another; at length a testy creditor sued him; his other creditors followed the example, and the unfortunate man saw all the dogs of the law let loose on him at once. He had not borne his prosperity calmly, and it could not therefore be expected that he should show himself a stoic under misfortune. He grew moody and testy, and a kind of instinct drove him again to ramble in the woods without either his rifle or his dogs, as was his wont in the days of his youth and his deformity.

One evening, as he was returning, a little after sunset, he chanced to pass slowly under the boughs of the great oak. He was thinking that on the whole he had little reason to thank the kindness of his super-natural friend. "She has made me a handsome fellow," thought he, "but what of that? If I had not been handsome, I should not have run into expenses that have made me poor. A man may as well be miserable from deformity as from poverty." At that very moment, a sweet, low voice, from the boughs of the tree, the well-remembered voice that three years before he had heard at nightfall on that very spot, articulated his name. He looked up, and saw the same calm features of unearthly loveliness and youth, with a smile playing about the beautiful mouth.

"I know thy thoughts, Caspar," said the apparition, "and thy misfortunes, and it shall not be my fault if thou art not happy. Dig on the north side of the trunk of this tree, just under the extremity of that long branch which points towards the ground, and there thou wilt find what, if thou art reasonable, will suffice thy wishes. Replace the earth carefully."

Caspar was of too impatient a temperament to defer for a moment the enjoyment of his good fortune. He went immediately for a spade. On his return he again looked up to the place where he had beheld the vision, but he saw only the brown bark of the tree visible in a strong gleam of twilight, and the neighbouring boughs and foliage moving and murmuring in the night-wind that was just beginning to rise. He turned up the earth at the spot which had been pointed out to him, and took out a large jar of money, and then shovelled back the mould; and pressed the turf into its place.

On examining the coins in the jar, they proved to be Spanish and Portuguese gold pieces of a pretty ancient date, all of them at least half a century old, some still older. Among the many persons from whom I have gathered the particulars of the tradition I am recording, I have not met with one who could satisfactorily explain the circumstance of the money being found in that place. It could not be the coinage of the apparition, for it was not to be supposed that she was the proprietor of a mint, and if she were, why should the coins be so old? As to the suggestion that it was buried there by Captain Kidd, the pirate, I do not think it worthy of notice, for I hold it certain that he concealed the money elsewhere, though it is not for my interest, at present, to reveal the particular spot. Besides, what should the Captain be doing in the woods of Pennsylvania, more than a hundred miles from the sea coast?

Caspar, however, cared not when the pieces were coined, nor by whom; he was not accustomed to speculate upon his good fortune, but to enjoy it. He held that, if there is any pleasure in the mere exercise of speculation, there is as much opportunity for it afforded by bad luck as by good, and he chose not to confound things which appeared to him so completely different. After paying off all his creditors, he gave a grand entertainment at his house, to which all his neighbours, for several miles round, were invited, and among the rest the testy creditor who had set the example of bringing a process against him. This fellow got as drunk as a lord on the whiskey of the man, whom, a few weeks ago, he would have ruined, and hugged his generous entertainer with tears in his eyes. As he was altogether too far gone to find his own way home, Caspar ordered out his great Pennsylvania wagon, drawn by two spirited horses, and driven by a shining-faced black fellow; the maudlin hero was lifted into the hinder seat, and nodding majestically as he went, was whirled home in that sublime condition.

It took less than half the gold of which Caspar became possessed in this extraordinary way, to satisfy all his debts; and the sight of the remainder, blinking and smiling in the capacious jar, was not likely to suggest to his mind any very strong motives for leaving off his habits of idleness and expense. His only study seemed how to get rid of his money, and in this laudable design fortune seemed willing to assist him.

About this time, Nicholas Vadokin, the schoolmaster who had penned the unfortunate epistle of Caspar to Adelaide, having saved a little money by his vocation, set up shop in the neighbourhood, which he furnished from Philadelphia with dry goods, and groceries, and all that miscellaneous collection of merchandise to be found in the store of a country trader. Nicholas was a cunning Hanoverian, with a shrewd hazel eye and brassy complexion. He was a prompt, ready-spoken man, who could turn his hand to anything, and having come to the United States to make his fortune, he would have thought himself convicted of want of perseverance and enterprise had he suffered himself to be diverted from his object by any trifling scruples of conscience. For four years he had flogged the children of the place for a livelihood, and he now resolved to try whether any thing could be made by fawning on their parents.

To Mr. Buckel, as the richest man in the neighbourhood, he was particularly attentive and obsequious. He always offered him a glass of bad wine whenever he came to his shop; talked to him of his wealth, his horses, his wagon, and his dogs; listened with profound interest to long stories of his hunting exploits; and though he scorned to flatter a man to his face, hinted that he ought to be a candidate for the Pennsylvania House of Representatives. He was so conscientious as to let him have all the goods for which he had occasion, at first cost; and whenever one of his loaded wagons arrived from Philadelphia, he never failed to take his patron aside, and tell him of such and such articles, which he had purchased expressly on his account—all which, the good natured Caspar was always sure to take off his hands.

Caspar soon came to be a daily frequenter of the shop, and he never called without making a purchase; for the ingenious Nicholas had always a reason for his taking almost every article he had. One thing was necessary, another convenient, one was fashionable, another indispensable to a man of his fortune and character; this was wonderfully cheap, and that wonderfully rare; and how could he refuse to be guided by the advice of his excellent and disinterested friend, who was so attentive to his convenience, and who let him have every thing at cost. In a short time, Caspar found the bottom of his jar; his money was gone, but his habits of expense were not easily shaken off; and, being pressed for cash, he applied to his friend Nicholas. Nicholas showed himself truly his friend; for he counted out to him the sum he wanted, with many smiles and protestations of delight at being able to do him a service, and took a mortgage of his estate.

The story of the mortgage soon took air, and immediately afterwards, Caspar, finding himself without money, found himself without credit also. In his embarrassment he again went to Nicholas for assistance, but his disinterested friend unfortunately had not the means of helping him further. A day or two after he called at the shop for the purpose of beginning a new score; but Nicholas informed him, with a very solemn look, that although there was no man in the world whom he would go farther to serve than his very good friend Mr. Buckel, yet his duty to his family obliged him to give credit to those only whose circumstances justified the expectation that they would pay; he added, however, that he should be exceedingly happy to supply him with any thing he wanted, for ready cash. Caspar stood for a moment as if thunderstruck, and the next, his rage prevailing over his astonishment, he levelled a blow at the Hanoverian, which would infallibly have knocked him down, had he not wisely avoided it by ducking under the counter.

Caspar returned home to digest his mortification as he could, and the blue devils followed him and fastened upon him. He felt the thirst of Tantalus, a continual craving for expense, with no means of satisfying it; it seemed to him as if all the rest of the world were rolling in wealth, buying and selling, driving fine horses, and feasting each other like princes, while he, poor fellow, had not a beggarly doit to spend. He grew meagre and hollow-eyed, and walked about with his hands in his pockets, looking vacantly at the geese nipping the grass before his door, and the hens wallowing in the sand of the road, and jerking it over their backs with their wings. At last he thought of the vision he had seen in the oak. "I will see her again," thought he; "who knows but she may relieve me a second time?"

He set off for the tree that very evening. It was an October night, and he lingered under it till the grass grew silvery with the frost, but she did not appear. The next evening he repaired to the same spot, and looked with a still more intense anxiety for her appearance, but he saw only the boughs struggling with the wind, and the dropping leaves. The third evening he was more successful; she was there, but her look was sad and reproachful. At times the gusts that swept by would rudely toss her hair above her forehead and against the trunk of the tree; and then, as they subsided, it would fall down again on each side of her fine countenance.

"I had hoped, Caspar," said the vision, with a mournful voice, that seemed like an articulate sigh, "to have reserved for some more pressing need of thine, the last favour that is in my power to bestow upon thee. I have observed thy nightly visits to my shade; I know thy motive; I know that thou wilt be unhappy if my bounty is withheld; and I cannot forget that thou wast born under my boughs, and that thy intercession has preserved me from the axe. Between the two roots that diverge eastward from my trunk, thou wilt find a portion of what the children of men value more than all the other gifts of heaven. Replace the turf over my roots, and remember that this is the last of my benefits."

Caspar dug eagerly in the spot, for he had been provident enough to bring his spade with him, and joyfully carried home a jar of money of the same figure and capacity with the former.

It were long to tell by what methods Caspar contrived to get rid of the second donation of the lady of the oak. To do him justice, he set out with the firmest resolutions of frugality and economy, and actually kept the gold by him three days without touching a moidore. But when he came to raise the mortgage of his friend Nicholas, and to satisfy some other debts that were a little troublesome, the habit of paying out money, being once re-admitted, obstinately kept possession. His old propensity to extravagance returned upon him with a violence that swept all his resolutions away. It is true, that when he saw his finances nearly exhausted, he made some praiseworthy attempts to repair them. It is whispered that he gambled a little with certain smooth-spoken, well-dressed emigrants from the country of his fathers; and it is very certain that he bought lottery tickets, drew blanks, bought others, and had the satisfaction of drawing an additional number of blanks.

(I have often thought that it was a thousand pities that Caspar did not live in these blessed times, and in this well-governed state of New-York, where the law refuses to license these pernicious institutions, and prohibits the sale of the tickets of all such as are established in other states. It is true, that the ghosts of old lotteries chartered long ago are raised, and meet you at every turn; that lottery offices are multiplied without number, and almost every tenth door holds out an invitation to try your luck; that the worthy and conscientious people who live, by decoying others into this legalized gambling, swarm all over our city, each provided with his poet, who indites his advertisement in the sweetest of rhymes—a circumstance conveying this most beautiful moral, little attended to, I fear, by the eager adventurer who buys the ticket— that he is paying his money for a song. I say it is a pity that Caspar had not lived in these blessed times, and in this blessed state; for although he might not have been prevented from engaging as deeply as he pleased in these beneficial speculations, he could not but have admired the wise and effectual measures taken to suppress them.)

Suffice it to say, that Caspar saw himself growing poor, and, as he had no taste for the pleasures of such a condition, he determined to make a desperate effort to shoot beyond the circle of the whirlpool that threatened to carry him down. He was well satisfied that he should get nothing by applying to the lady of the oak, but he could not help suspecting that there was more gold under her boughs. "The two jars," said he to himself, "were concealed in different places, both near the same tree, which served as a kind of mark by which to find them again; and who knows how many more are lying scattered about the same spot? I will search at least; if there is any gold there, it is a pity it should lie useless in the earth, and if there is not, I shall lose nothing."

The very next morning he loaded his black servant and another labourer with pick-axes, spades, and hoes, and sent them to dig about and under the tree, with instructions to bring him immediately what-ever curious or remarkable thing they might find there. He was ashamed to go to the spot himself, for he felt that he had abused the gifts of his benefactress, and was now repaying her kindness with ingratitude. In the evening the labourers returned, having found nothing but a few fragments of a glass bottle, and complained that the water from the rivulet that ran near the tree, soaked through the earth and filled the excavations they were making. Caspar ordered them to dam it up a few rods nearer its source, and turn it into a new channel.

It was July, and a severe drought prevailed all over the country. The pastures looked red and sun-burnt; the hardy house-plantain, before Caspar's door, rolled up its leaves like a segar; the birds were silent; the cattle drooped; nothing was cheerful and lively but the grasshoppers, who always swarm thickest, and chirp merriest, in dry seasons, and the poultry, who chased and caught them by the sides of the road. The poor oak, almost undermined and deprived of the moisture of its rivulet, was the saddest looking tree in the whole country; its leaves grew yellow and rusty, and dropped off one by one; and it is said that once, when Caspar was looking towards it from one of the back windows of his house, just as the twilight set in, he fancied he saw again that fair, sad face, among the boughs, and a white shadowy arm, beckoning him to approach. But he hardened his heart, and turned away from the sight, and the next morning his labourers went on with their task.

One afternoon, on a day of uncommon heat, as Caspar was engaged at a tavern in bargaining for a pair of horses, with a jockey who had come twenty miles on purpose to cheat him, the labourers were driven from their work by a furious tempest. The woods roared and bent in the violent wind and the heavy rain, and a thousand new streams were at once formed, which ran winding all over the open country, like so many serpents. The brook, that formerly ran by the oak, broke over the barrier which diverted it from its course, and coming down the hill, with a vast body of water, ploughed for itself a new channel through the excavations of Caspar's workmen, and completed the undermining of the tree. At last a strong gust took it by the top and laid it on its side, with its long roots sticking up in the air. Caspar's family beheld its fall from the windows.

Two hours afterwards there was a clear sky, and a bright sun shining on the glistening earth, and the wet roofs of Caspar's building were smoking in the warm rays. A little pot-bellied man, with an enormous hump on his shoulders, small, thin legs and arms, and hideous features, dressed in a suit of clothes that seemed to have been made for a man much taller and straighter than himself, the collar of his coat standing erect about a foot from his neck, entered the house, and began to issue his commands to the servants with an air of authority. At first they only smiled at his conduct, supposing him to be insane, and offered him some broken victuals and a cup of cider. At this he flew into a great rage, and swore he was Caspar Buckel himself, the master of the house. Finding that he grew troublesome, they sent for Mrs.

Buckel, who was beginning to talk soothingly to him, with a view of persuading him to leave the house, but what was her astonishment when the misshapen being insisted that he was her husband. Shocked and frightened at his proof of his madness, she ordered the labourer and the black fellow to put him out of the house, which they effected with some difficulty, while he struggled, scratched, bit, foamed at the mouth, and declared, with a thousand oaths, that he was Caspar Buckel, their master. When they had got him out of the door, and had disengaged themselves from him, the black gave him a stroke with the long horsewhip that he used in driving his master's horses, and calling out the dogs, set them upon him. The deformed creature scampered before them into a neighbouring wood, and then the negro called them off.

Caspar did not return that night, and the next morning Mrs. Buckel sent to the tavern to inquire for him, but without learning any thing satisfactory concerning him. The landlord recollected he was there, about the middle of the tempest, but could not say when he left the house; he mentioned, also, that after the sky began to clear, a little hunch-backed man had asked at his bar for a glass of whiskey, and having paid for it, immediately went away. As for the jockey, he had gone off with his horses just before the storm began, having been unable to drive such a bargain with Mr. Buckel as he wished.

Mrs. Buckel continued her searches and inquiries for six weary months, after which she concluded that her husband was dead, and remained disconsolate for six months longer. At the end of this period she gave her hand to a young fellow from New England, who had fallen in love with her plump, round face, and well stocked farm.

As for Caspar, he was never heard of again; but the old people say that the woods north of his widow's house are haunted at twilight by the figure of a hunch-backed little man, skipping over the fallen trees, and running into gloomy thickets as soon as your eye falls on him, as if to avoid the sight of man.

The Indian Spring

One of the adventures of my life upon which I have since oftenest reflected, and concerning which my imagination is most inclined to dispute the dictates of my reason, happened many years ago, when, quite a young man, I made an excursion into the interior of the state of New-York, and passed a few days in the region whose waters flow into the east branch of the Susquehannah. My readers will easily judge for themselves whether what I am going to relate can be accounted for from natural causes. For my own part, however, so vivid is the impression it has left upon my mind, and so difficult is it with me to distinguish my recollections of it from that of the absolute realities of my life, that I find it the easier belief to ascribe it to a cause above nature.

I think I have elsewhere intimated that I have great sympathy with believers in the supernatural. Theoretically, I am as much a philosopher, and have as little of what is commonly called superstition about me, as most persons of my acquaintance; but the luxury of a little superstition in practice, the strong and active play into which it calls the imagination, the fine thrill it sends through the veins, the alternate gushes of fear and courage that come over us when under its influence, are too agreeable a relief from the dull realities of the material world to be readily given up. My own individual experience also makes me indulgent to those whose credulity in these matters exceeds my own. Is it to be wondered at that the dogmas of philosophy should not gain credit when they have the testimony of our own senses against them? You say that this evidence is often counterfeited by the tricks of fancy, the hallucinations of the nerves, and by our very dreams. You are right–but who shall in all cases distinguish the false experience from the true?

The part of the country of which I am speaking had just been invaded by the footsteps of cultivation. Openings had been made here and there in the great natural forest, log houses had been built, the farmers were gathering in their first crops of tall grass, and the still taller harvests of wheat and rye stood up by the side of the woods in the clearings. It was then the month of June, and I sallied forth from my lodgings at a paltry log tavern to ramble in the woods with a friend of mine who had come with me from New-York. We set out amid the warblings of the birds, scarce waiting for the dew to be dried up from the herbage. I carried a fowling-piece on my shoulder; not that I meant to be the death of any living creature that fine morning, when everything seemed so happy, but because such a visible pretext for a stroll in the woods and fields satisfies at once the curiosity of those whom you meet, and saves you often a world of staring, and sometimes not a few impertinent questions. I hold it right and fair to kill game late in the autumn, when the animal has had his feast of fruits and nuts, and is left with a prospect of a long, hard, uncomfortable winter before him, and the dangers of being starved to death. But to take his life in the spring, or the beginning of summer, when he has so many fine sunny months of frolic and plenty before him—it is gratuitous cruelty, and I have ever religiously abstained from it.

My companion was much more corpulent than I, and as slow a walker as I was a fast one. However, he good-naturedly exerted himself to keep up with me, and I made more than one attempt to moderate my usual speed for his accommodation. The effort worried us both. At length he fairly gave out, and, bringing the butt of his fowling-piece smartly to the ground, stood still, with both hands grasping the muzzle.

"I beg," said he, "that you will go on at your own pace. I promise faithfully not to stir from the spot till you are fairly out of sight."

"But I am very willing to walk slower."

"No," rejoined my friend, "we did not set out together for the purpose of making each other uncomfortable, nor will we, if I can help it. Here we have been fretting and chafing each other for half an hour. Why, it is like yoking an ox with a race-horse. Go on, I beseech you, while I stop to recover my wind. I wish you a pleasant walk of it. I shall expect to see you back at our landlord's at one o' clock."

I took him at his word, and proceeded. I rambled through tall old groves clear of underwood, beside rivulets broken into little pools and cascades by rocks and fallen timber, along the edges of dark, shrubby swamps, and across sunny clearings, until I was tired. At length I came to a pleasant natural glade on the slope of a hill, and sat down under the shade of a tree to rest myself. It was a narrow opening in the woods, extending for some distance up the hill, and terminating in that quarter at the base of a ridge of rocks, above which rose the forest. At the lower end, near which I was, a spring rose up in a little hollow and formed a streamlet, which ran off under the trees. A most still, quiet nook it was, sheltered from all winds; the leaves were not waved, nor the grass bent by a breath of air, and the sun came down between the enclosing trees with so strong a heat that, except in the shade, I felt the warmth of the ground through the soles of my shoes.

As I lay with my head propped on my hand, and my elbow buried in a mass of herbage, my thoughts turned involuntarily upon the ancient inhabitants of these woods. Here, said I to myself, in this very spot, some Indian doubtless fixed his cabin; or haply some little neighborhood, the branch of a larger tribe, nestled in this sylvan enclosure. That circle of moldering timber is probably the remains of the wigwam of the last inhabitant, and that great vine which sprawls over it was probably once supported by its walls, and, when they were abandoned and decaying, dragged them to the ground, as many a parasite has done by his credulous benefactor. Here the Indian woman planted her squashes and tended her maize; here the Indian father brought forth his boys to try their bows, and aim their little tomahawks at the trees, teaching—for even in the solemnity of my feelings I could not forbear the pun—teaching

"The young idea how to shoot."

That spring, which gushes up so brightly and abundantly from the ground, yielded them, when their exercise was over, a beverage never mingled with the liquid poisons of the civilized world, and gave its cresses to season the simple repast. Gradually my imagination became both awed and kindled by these reflections. I felt rebuked by the wild genius of a place familiar for centuries only with the race of red men and hunters, and I almost expected to see some Indian, with his tomahawk and bow, walk up to me and ask me what I did there.

My thoughts were diverted from this subject by my eyes falling upon an earth-newt, as red as fire, crawling lazily and with an almost imperceptible motion over the grass. I yawned by a sort of sympathy with the sluggish creature, and, oppressed with fatigue and heat, for the sun was getting high, loosened my cravat and stretched out my legs to an easier position. All at once I found myself growing drowsy, my eyelids dropping involuntarily, my eyes rolling in their sockets with a laborious attempt to keep themselves open, and the landscape swimming and whirling before me, as if I saw it in a mirror suspended by a loose string and waving in the wind. Once or twice the scene was entirely lost for a moment to my vision, and I perceived that I had actually been asleep. It struck me that I might be better employed than in taking a nap at that time of day, and, accordingly, I rose and walked across the glade until I came to the foot of the rocks at the upper end of it, when I turned to take another look at the pleasant and quiet spot. Judge of my astonishment when I actually beheld, standing by the very circle of rubbish near which I had been reposing, and which I had taken for the remains of a wigwam, an Indian, a real Indian, the very incarnation of the images that had been floating in my fancy. I will not say that I did not spring from the ground when the figure met my eye—so sudden and startling was the shock it gave me. He was not one of that degenerate kind which I had seen in various parts of the country wearing hats, frock-coats, pantaloons, and Dutch blankets, but was dressed in the original garb of his nation. A covering of skin was wrapped about his loins, a mantle of the same was flung loosely over his shoulders, and his legs were bare from the middle of the thigh down to his ornamented moccasons. A single tuft of stiff, black hair on the top of his head, from which the rest was carefully plucked, was mingled with the gaudy plumage of different birds; a bow and a bundle of arrows peeped over his shoulder; a necklace of bears' claws hung down upon his breast; his right hand carried a tomahawk, and the fingers of his left were firmly closed, like those of one whose physical vigor and resoluteness of purpose suffered not the least muscle of his frame to relax for a moment. Notwithstanding the distance at which he stood, and which might be a hundred paces at least, I saw his whole figure, even to the minutest article of dress, with what seemed to me an unnatural distinctness. His countenance had that expression which has been so often remarked upon as peculiar to the aborigines of our country—a settled look of sullenness, sadness, and suspicion, as if when moulded by nature it had been visibly stamped with the presentiment of the decline and disappearance of their race. The features were strongly marked, hard, and stern; high cheekbones, a broad forehead, an aquiline nose, garnished with an oblong piece of burnished copper; a mouth, somewhat wide, between a parenthesis of furrows, and a bony and fleshless chin. But then his eyes—such eyes I have never seen—distant as they were from me, they seemed close to my own, and to ray out an unpleasant brightness from their depths, like twin stars of evil omen. Their influence unstrung all my sinews, and a gush of sudden and almost suffocating heat came over my whole frame. I averted my look instantly and fixed it upon the feet of the savage, shod with their long moccasons, and standing motionless among the thick weeds; but could not keep it there. Again my eyes returned upward; again they encountered his, glittering in the midst of that calm, sullen face, and again that oppressive, stifling sensation came over me. It was natural that I should feel an impulse to remove from so unpleasant a neighborhood; I therefore shouldered my fowling-piece, climbed the rock before me, and penetrated into the woods. As I proceeded, the idea took possession of me that I was followed by the Indian, and I walked pretty fast in order to shake it off; but I found this impossible. I had got into a state of fidgety, nervous excitement, and it seemed to me that I felt the rays of those bright, unnatural eyes on my shoulders, my back, my arms, and even my hands, as I flung them back in walking. At length I looked back, and, notwithstanding I half expected to see him, I was scarcely less surprised than at first, when I beheld the same figure, just at the same distance, standing motionless as then, his bright eyes gleaming upon me between the trunks of the trees. A third time I felt that flush of dissolving heat, and a violent sweat broke out all over me. I have heard of the cold, clammy sweat of fear; mine was not of that temperature; it was as the warmest summer rain, warm and free and profuse as the current of brooks in the hottest and moistest season of dog days. I walked on, keeping my sight fixed on the strange apparition. It did not seem to move, and, as I proceeded, gradually diminished by the natural effect of distance until I could scarcely distinguish it among the thick trunks and boughs of the forest. Happening to avert my eyes for a moment, I saw, as I turned again to the spot, that the figure had swiftly and silently gained upon me, and was now at the same distance as when I first beheld it. A clearing lay before me. I saw the sunshine and the grass between the trunks of the trees, and, rushing forward, found myself under the open sky, and felt relieved by a freer air. I looked back, and nothing was to be seen of my pursuer. A small log-house stood in the open space, with a well beside it, and a tall, rude machine of the kind they call a well-sweep leaning over it, loaded with a bucket at one end and a heavy stone at the other. A boy of about twelve years of age was drawing water. The sight of a human habitation, and a habitation of white men, was a welcome one to me; and, tormented as I was with heat and thirst, I rejoiced at the prospect of refreshing myself with a draught of the cool, pure element. Accordingly, I made for the well, and arrived at it just as the boy was pouring the contents of the bucket into a large stone pitcher. "You will give me a taste of the water?" said I to him.

"And welcome," replied the boy, "if you'll drink out of the pitcher, for the mug is broke, and we haven't got any glasses."

I stooped, and, raising the heavy vessel to my lips, took a copious draught from the brim, where the cold water was yet sparkling with the bubbles raised by pouring it from the bucket. "Your water is very fine," said I, when I had recovered my breath.

"Yes, but not so fine as you'll get at the Indian spring," rejoined he. "That's the best water in all the country—the clearest, the coldest, and the sweetest. Father always sends me to the Indian spring when he wants the best water, when uncle comes up from York, or the minister makes us a visit."

"What is it that you call the Indian spring?" I inquired.

"Oh, I guess you must have passed it, by the way you came. Didn't you see a spring of water, east of a ledge of rocks, in a pretty spot of ground where there were no trees?"

"I believe I saw something of the kind," said I, recollecting the glade in which I had thrown myself to rest shortly before, and its fountain.

"That was the Indian spring; and, if you took notice, you must have seen some old logs and sticks lying in a heap, and a few stones that look as if there had been fire on them. It was thought that an Indian family lived there before the country was settled by our people."

"Are there any Indians in this neighborhood at present?" I inquired, with some eagerness.

"Oh, no, indeed; they are gone to the west'ard, so they say, though I am not big enough to know anything about it. It was before father came into the country—long before. The only Indian I ever saw was Jemmy Sunkum, who came about last summer, selling brooms and begging cider."

"A tall, spare, strong-looking man, was he?" asked I, "dressed in skins, and carrying a bow?" my thoughts naturally recurring to the figure I had just seen.

The boy grinned. "Not much taller than I am, and as fat as a woodchuck; and as for the skins he wore, I never see any but his own through the holes of his trousers, unless it be a squirrel-skin that he carried his tobacco and loose change in. He wore an old hat with the crown torn out, and had lost one of his eyes—they say it was by drinking so much cider. Father swapped an old pair of pantaloons with him for a broom. But I must take this pitcher to father, who is at work in the corn-field yonder; so good-morning to you, sir."

The lad tripped away, whistling, and I sat down on one of the broad, flat stones by the well-side, under the shade of a young tree of the kind commonly called yellow willow, which in a year or two shoots up from a slip of the size of a man's finger into a fine, shapely, overshadowing tree. I laid my hat and gun by my side and wiped my hot and sweaty forehead, upon which the wind, that swayed to and fro the long, flexible, depending branches, breathed with a luxurious coolness.

The Indian I have seen cannot be the one that the boy means, said I to myself, nor probably any other of which the inhabitants know anything. That fine, majestic savage is a very different being from the fat, one-eyed vagabond in the ragged trousers that the lad speaks of. It is probably some ancient inhabitant of the place, returned from the forest of the distant West to visit the scenes of his childhood. But what could he mean by following me in this manner, and why should he keep his eye fixed on me so strangely? As I said this, I looked along the forest I had just quitted, examining it carefully and with an eye sharpened by the excited state of my imagination, to see if I could discover anything of my late pursuer. All was quiet and motionless. I heard the bee as he flew by heavily from the cucumber-flowers in the garden near me, and the hum of the busy wheel from the open windows of the cottage; but face or form of human being I saw not. I replaced my hat on my head and my gun on my shoulder, crossed the clearing, and entered the opposite wood, intending to return home by a kind of circuit, for I did not care again to encounter the savage, whose demeanor was so mysterious.

I had proceeded but a few rods, when, a mingled sensation of uneasiness and curiosity inducing me to look over my shoulder, I started to behold the very figure, whose sight I was endeavoring to avoid, just entering the forest—the same brawny shoulders clad with skins, the same sad, stern, suspicious countenance, the same bright eyes thrilling and scorching me with their light. Again I felt that indescribable sensation of discomfort and heat, and the perspiration, which had ceased to flow while I sat by the well, again gushed forth from every pore. Involuntarily I stopped short. What was this being, and why should he dog my steps in this strange manner? What were his designs, pacific or hostile? and what method should I take to rid myself of his pursuit? I had tried walking away from him without effect; should I now adopt the expedient of walking up to him and asking his business? The thought struck me that, if his designs were malevolent, this step might bring me into danger—he was well armed with a tomahawk and arrows, and who could tell the force and certainty of his aim? This fear, on reflection, I rejected as groundless and unmanly; for what cause had he to seek my life? It was but prudent, however, to prepare myself for the worst that could happen. I therefore examined my priming, and, as I had nothing but small bird-shot with me, I kicked up the dry leaves from the earth under my feet, and, selecting a handful of the smallest, smoothest, and roundest pebbles from among the gravel, put two or three of them into the muzzle, and lodged the rest in my pocket. As I turned, there was that face still, at the very edge of the forest, glaring steadily upon me, and watching my operations with the unchanging, stony, stoical expression of the Indian race. I replaced the piece on my shoulder, and advanced toward it. Scarcely had I gone three paces when it suddenly disappeared behind the huge old trunk of an old buttonwood, or plane-tree, that stood just in the edge of the clearing. I approached the tree; there was no living thing behind it or near it. I looked out into the clearing, and scanned its whole extent for the object of my search, but in vain. There was the cottage, in which the wheel was still humming, and the well with its young willow waving restlessly over it. The clearing was long and narrow, and widened away toward the south, where was a field of Indian corn, in which I could distinguish my friend, the lad who had given me the water, in company with a man who, I suppose, was his father, diligently engaged in hoeing the corn; and at intervals I could hear the click of their hoes against the stones. Nothing else was to be seen, nothing else to be heard. I turned and searched the bushes about me; nothing was there. I looked up into the old plane-tree above my head; the clean and handsomely divided branches, speckled with white, guided my eye far into the very last of their verdurous recesses, but no creature, not even a bird, was to be seen there. Strange as it may seem, I found myself refreshed and cooled by this search, and relieved from the burning and suffocating heat that I felt while the eye of the savage rested upon me. My perplexity was, however, anything but lessened; and I resolved to pursue my way home with as little delay as possible, and spell out, if I could, the mystery at my leisure. Accordingly, I plunged again into the woods, and, after proceeding a little way, began to change my course, in a direction which I judged must bring me to the spot where I had rested in the Indian glade near the spring, from which I doubted not I could find my way home without difficulty. As I proceeded, the heat of the day seemed to grow more and more oppressive. There was shade about me and over my head—thick shade of oak, maple, and walnut—but it seemed to me as if beams of the hottest midsummer sun were beating upon my back and scorching the skin of my neck. I turned my head, and there again stood the Indian, with that eternal, intolerable glare of the eyes. I stopped not, but went on with a quicker pace. My face was flushed, my brow throbbed audibly, my head ached, the veins in my hands were swollen till they looked like ropes, and the sweat dropped from my hair like rain. A fine brook crossed my way, clear as diamond, full to the very brim, and sending up a cool vapor from its surface that promised for the grateful temperature of its waters. I longed to strip off my clothes, and lay myself down in its bed at full length, and steep my burning limbs in its current. Just then I remembered the story of Tam o' Shanter pursued by witches, and saved by crossing a running stream. If there be any witchcraft in this thing, said I to myself, it will not follow me beyond this brook. I was ashamed of the thought as it crossed my mind, but I leaped the brook notwithstanding, and hurried on. Turning afterward to observe the effect of my precaution, I saw the savage standing in the midst of the very current, the bright water flowing round his copper-colored ankles. The sight was as vexatious as it was singular, and did not by any means diminish my haste. A little opening, where the trees had been cut down and the ground sown with European grasses, came in my way, and I entered it. In this spot the red and white clover grew rankly, and blossomed side by side with columbine and cranesbill, the natives of the soil—flowers and verdure the more striking in their beauty for the unsightly and blackened stumps of trees standing thick among them—a sweet, still nook, a perpetual concert of humming-birds and bees, and a thousand beautiful winged insects, for which our common speech has no name, and exhaling from the herbage an almost overpowering stream of fragrance. I no longer saw my pursuer. What could this mean? Was this figure some restless shadow, that could haunt only its ancient wilderness, and was excluded from every spot reclaimed and cultivated by the white man? I took advantage of this respite to wipe my face and forehead; I unbuttoned my waistcoat, took off my cravat and put it in my pocket, threw back the collar of my coat from my shoulders, fanned myself awhile with my hat, and then went on. Soon after I again entered the wood, I perceived with surprise that my tormentor had gained upon me. He was twice as near to me as when I first saw him, and the strange light that seemed to shoot from his eyes was more intense and insufferable than ever. I was in a part of the forest which was thickly strewn with the fallen trunks of trees, wrenched up, as it seemed to me, long ago by some mighty wind. I hastened on, leaping from one to another, occasionally looking back at my pursuer. The air in my face, as I flew forward, seemed as if issuing from the mouth of a furnace. In leaping upon a spot where the earth was moist and soft, one of my shoes remained embedded fast in the soil. It is an old one, said I to myself; I shall be lighter and cooler without it. Immediately the low branch of a tree struck my hat from my head as I rushed onward. No matter, thought I–I will send a boy to look for it in the morning. As I sprang from a rock my other shoe flew off, and dropped on the ground before me; I caught it up without stopping, and jerked it over my head with all my strength at the savage behind me. When I next looked back, I saw that he had decked himself with my spoils. He had strung both my shoes to his necklace of bears' claws, and had crowded down my hat upon his head over that tuft of long black hair mingled with feathers, the ends of which stood out under the brim in front, forming a wild, grotesque shade to those strangely bright eyes. Still I went on, and, in springing upon a log covered with green moss, and moist and slimy with decay, my foot slipped, and I could only keep from falling by dropping the fowling-piece I carried. I did not stop to pick it up, and the next instant it was upon the shoulder of the Indian, or demon, that chased me. I darted forward, panting, glowing, perspiring, ready to sink to the earth with heat and fatigue, until suddenly I found myself on the edge of that ridge of rocks which rose above the Indian glade, where I had thrown myself to rest under a tree in the morning, before my steps had been dogged by the savage. The whole scene lay beneath my feet, the spring, the ruins of the wigwam, the tree under which I reclined. A single desperate leap took me far down into the glade below me, and a few rapid strides brought me to the very spot where I had been reposing, and where the pressure of my form still remained on the grass. A shrill, wild shout, with which the woods rang in sharp echoes, rose upon the air, and instantly I perceived that my pursuer had leaped also, and was at my side, and had seized me with a strong and sudden grip that shook every fibre of my frame. A strange darkness came over all visible objects, and I sank to the ground.

An interval of insensibility followed, the duration of which I have no means of computing, and from which I was at last aroused by noises near me, and by motions of my body produced by some impulse from without. I opened my eyes on the very spot where I remembered to have reclined in the morning. My hat was off, my hair and clothes were steeped in sweat, my fowling-piece and shoes lay within a few feet of me, but scattered in different directions. My friend, who had accompanied me at the outset of my ramble, was shaking me by the shoulder, bawling my name in my ear, and asking me if I meant to lie there all day. I sat up, and found that the shade of the tree under which I was had shifted many feet from its original place, and that I was lying exposed to the burning beams of the sun. My old acquaintance, the red earth-newt, had made great progress in the grass, having advanced at least a yard from the place where I remembered to have seen him when I was beginning to grow drowsy, before my adventure with the savage. My friend complained that he had been looking for me for more than an hour, and hallooing himself hoarse without effect, and that he was sure we should be late for dinner.

I said nothing to my companion about what had happened until the next day, when I ventured to relate a part of the strange series of real or imaginary circumstances connected with my ramble. He laughed at the earnestness of my manner, and very promptly and flippantly said it was nothing but a dream. My readers may possibly be of the same opinion; and I myself when in a philosophical mood, incline to this way of accounting for the matter. At other times, however, when I recall to mind the various images and feelings of that time, deeply and distinctly engraved on my memory, I find nothing in them which should lead me to class them with the illusions of sleep, and nothing to distinguish them from the waking experience of my life.

Bryant As Critic

THE CHALLENGE OF CREATING A NATIONAL LITERARY TRADITION IN A MODERN TIME

Extracts from *Originality and Imitation*

. . . . There is no warrant for the notion, maintained by some, that the first poets in any language were great poets, or that, whatever their rank, they did not learn their art from the great poets in other languages. It might as well be expected that a self-taught architect would arise in a country whose inhabitants live in caves, and, without models or instruction, raise the majestic Parthenon and pile up St. Peter's into the clouds.

That there were poets in the English language before Chaucer, some of whom were not unworthy to be his predecessors, is attested by extant monuments of their verse; and, if there had not been, he might have learned his art from the polished poets of Italy, whom he studied and loved. Italy had versifiers before Dante, and, if they were not his masters, he at least found masters in the harmonious poets of a kindred dialect, the Provençal. In the Provençal language, the earliest of the cultivated tongues of modern Europe, there arose no great poet. The reason was that their literature had scarcely been brought to that degree of perfection which produces the finest specimens of poetry when the hour of its decline had come. It possessed, it is true, authors innumerable, revivers of the same art, enrichers of the same idiom, and polishers of the same system of versification, yet they never looked for models out of their own literature; they did not study the remains of ancient poetry to avail themselves of its riches; they confined themselves to such improvements and enlargements of the art as were made among themselves; and therefore their progress, though wonderful for the circumstances in which they were placed, was yet limited in comparison with that of those nations who have had access to the treasures they neglected. ....

At the present day, however, a writer of poems writes in a language which preceding poets have polished, refined, and filled with forcible, graceful, and musical expressions. He is not only taught by them to overcome the difficulties of rhythmical construction, but he is shown, as it were, the secrets of the mechanism by which he moves the mind of his reader; he is shown ways of kindling the imagination and of interesting the passions which his own sagacity might never have discovered; his mind is filled with the beauty of their sentiments, and their enthusiasm is breathed into his soul. He owes much, also, to his contemporaries as well as to those who have gone before him. He reads their works, and whatever excellence he beholds in them, inspires him with a strong desire to rival it—stronger, perhaps, than that excited by the writings of his predecessors; for such is our reverence for the dead that we are willing to concede to them that superiority which we are anxious snatch from the living. Even if he should refuse to read the writings of his brethren, he cannot escape the action of their minds on his own. He necessarily comes to partake somewhat of the character of their genius, which is impressed not only on all contemporary literature, but even on the daily thoughts of those with whom he associates. .... Deprive an author of these advantages, and what sort of poetry does any one imagine that he would produce? I dare say it would be sufficiently original, but who will affirm that it could be read?

The poet must do precisely what is done by the mathematician, who takes up his science where his predecessors have left it, and pushes its limits as much farther, and makes as many new applications of its principles, as he can. He must found himself on the excellence already attained in his art, and if, in addition to this, he delights us with new modes of sublimity, of beauty, and of human emotion, he deserves the praise of originality and of genius. If he has nothing of all this, he is entitled to no other honor than belongs to him who keeps alive the practice of a delightful and beautiful art.

This very necessity, however, of a certain degree of dependence upon models in poetry has at some periods led into an opposite fault to the inordinate desire of originality. The student, instead of copying nature with the aid of knowledge derived from these models, has been induced to make them the original, from which the copy was to be drawn. He has been led to take an imperfect work—and all human works are imperfect—as the standard of perfection, and to dwell upon it with such reverence that he comes to see beauties where no beauties are, and excellence in place of positive defects. Thus the study of poetry, which should encourage the free and unlimited aspirations of the mind after all that is noble and beautiful, has been perverted into a contrivance to chill and repress them. ...

It is long since the authority of great names was disregarded in matters of science. Ages ago the schools shook themselves loose from the fetters of Aristotle. He no more now delivers the oracles of philosophy than the priests of Apollo deliver the oracles of religion. Why should the chains of authority be worn any longer by the heart and the imagination than by the reason? This is a question which the age has already answered. The genius of modern times has gone out in every direction in search of originality. Its ardor has not always been compensated by the discovery of its object, but under its auspices a fresh, vigorous, and highly original poetry has grown up. The fertile soil of modern literature has thrown up, it is true, weeds among the flowers, but the flowers are of immortal bloom and fragrance, and the weeds are soon outworn. It is no longer necessary that a narrative poem should be written on the model of the ancient epic; a lyric composition is not relished the more, perhaps not so much, for being Pindaric or Horatian; and it is not required that a satire should remind the reader of Juvenal. It is enough for the age if beautiful diction, glowing imagery, strong emotion, and fine thought are so combined as to give them their fullest effect upon the mind. The end of poetry is then attained, no matter by what system of rules. ....

But when once a tame and frigid taste has possessed the tribe of poets, when all their powers are employed in servilely copying the works of their predecessors, it is not only impossible that any great work should be produced among them, but the period of a literary reformation, of the awakening of genius, is postponed to a distant futurity. It is the quality of such a state of literature, by the imposing precision of its rules and the ridicule it throws on everything out of its own beaten track, to perpetuate itself indefinitely. The happy appearance of some extraordinary genius, educated under different influences than those operating on the age, and compelling admiration by the force of his talents; or, perhaps, some great moral or political revolution, by unsettling old opinions and familiarizing men to daring speculations—can alone have any effect to remove it.

Poetry's Relation to Our Age and Country

An opinion prevails, which neither wants the support of respectable names nor of plausible reasonings, that the art of poetry, in common with its sister arts, painting and sculpture, cannot in the present age be cultivated with the same degree of success as formerly. It has been supposed that the progress of reason, of science, and of the useful arts has a tendency to narrow the sphere of the imagination, and to repress the enthusiasm of the affections. Poetry, it is alleged, whose office it was to nurse the infancy of the human race, and to give it its first lessons of wisdom, having fulfilled the part to which she was appointed, now resigns her charge to severer instructors. Others, again, refining upon this idea, maintain that not only the age in which we live must fail to produce anything to rival the productions of the ancient masters of song, but that our own country, of all parts of the globe, is likely to remain the most distant from such a distinction.

Our citizens are held to possess, in a remarkable degree, the heedful, calculating, prosaic spirit of the age, while our country is decried as peculiarly barren of the materials of poetry. The scenery of our land these reasoners admit to be beautiful, but they urge that it is the beauty of a face without expression, that it wants the associations of tradition which are the soul and interest of scenery; that it wants the national superstitions which linger yet in every district in Europe, and the legends of distant and dark ages and of wild and unsettled times of which the old world reminds you at every step. Nor can our country, they say, ever be more fruitful of these materials than at present For this is not an age to give birth to new superstitions, but to explode and root out old, however harmless and agreeable they may be, while half the world is already wondering how little the other half will finally believe. Is it likely, then, that a multitude of interesting traditions will spring up in our land to ally themselves with every mountain, every hill, every forest, every river, and every tributary brook? There may be some passages of our early history which associate themselves with particular places, but the argument is that the number of these will never be greatly augmented. The genius of our nation is quiet and commercial. Our people are too much in love with peace and gain, the state of society is too settled, and the laws too well enforced and respected, to allow of wild and strange adventures. There is no romance either in our character, our history, or our condition of society; and, therefore, it is neither likely to encourage poetry, nor capable of supplying it with those materials–materials drawn from domestic traditions and manners–which render it popular.

If these views of the tendency of the present age, and the state of things in our own country, are to be received as true, it must be acknowledged that they are not only exceedingly discouraging to those who make national literature a matter of pride, but, what is worse, that they go far toward causing that very inferiority on which they so strongly insist. Not that there is any danger that the demand for contemporary poetry will entirely cease. Verses have always been, and always will be written, and will always find readers; but it is of some consequence that they should be good verses, that they should be the healthful and beneficial influences which I consider belonging to the highest productions of the art; not feebly and imperfectly, but fully and effectually.

If, however, excellence in any art is believed to be unattainable, it will never be attained. There is, indeed, no harm in representing it as it really is, in literature as in every other pursuit, as rare and difficult, for by this means they who aspire to it are incited to more vigorous exertions. The mind of man glories in nothing more than in struggling successfully with difficulty, and nothing more excites our interest and admiration than the view of this struggle and triumph. The distinction of having done what few are able to do is the more enviable from its unfrequency, and attracts a multitude of competitors who catch each other's ardor and imitate each other's diligence. But if you go a step farther, and persuade those who are actuated by a generous ambition that this difficulty amounts to an impossibility, you extinguish their zeal at once. You destroy hope, and with it strength; you drive from the attempt those who were most likely and most worthy to succeed, and you put in their place a crowd of inferior contestants, satisfied with a low measure of excellence, and incapable of apprehending anything higher. Should, then, the views of this subject of which I have spoken be untrue, we may occasion much mischief by embracing them; and it becomes us, before we adopt them, to give them an attentive examination, and to be perfectly satisfied of their soundness.

But, if it be a fact that poetry in the present age is unable to attain the same degree of excellence as formerly, it cannot certainly be ascribed to any change in the original and natural faculties and dispositions of mind by which it is produced and by which it is enjoyed. The theory that men have degenerated in their mental powers and moral temperament is even more absurd than the notion of a decline in their physical strength and is too fanciful to be combated by grave reasoning. It would be difficult, I fancy, to persuade the easiest credulity that the imagination of man has become, with the lapse of ages, less active and less capable of shaping the materials at its command into pictures of majesty and beauty. Is anybody whimsical enough to suppose that the years that have passed since the days of Homer have made men's hearts cold and insensible or deadened the delicacy of their moral perceptions, or rendered them less susceptible of cultivation? All the sources of poetry in the mind, and all the qualities to which it owes its power over the mind, are assuredly left us. Degeneracy, if it has taken place, must be owing to one of two things—either to the absence of those circumstances which, in former times, developed and cherished the poetical faculty to an extraordinary degree, or to the existence of other intellectual interests which, in the present age, tend to repress its natural exercise.

What, then, were the circumstances which fostered the art of poetry in ancient times? They have been defined to be the mystery impressed on all the operations of nature as yet not investigated and traced to their laws—the beautiful systems of ancient mythology, and, after their extinction, the superstitions that linger like ghosts in the twilight of a later age. Let us examine separately each of these alleged advantages. That there is something in whatever is unknown and inscrutable which strongly excites the imagination and awes the heart, particularly when connected with things of unusual vastness and grandeur, is not to be denied. But I deny that much of this mystery is apparent to an ignorant age, and I maintain that no small degree of inquiry and illumination is necessary to enable the mind to perceive it. He who takes all things to be as they appear, who supposes the earth to be a great plain, the sun a moving ball of fire, the heavens a vault of sapphire, and the stars a multitude of little flames lighted up in its arches–what does he think of mysteries, or care for them? But enlighten him a little further. Teach him that the earth is an immense sphere; that the wide land whose bounds he knows so imperfectly is an isle in the great oceans that flow all over it; talk to him of the boundlessness of the skies, and the army of worlds that move through them–and, by means of the knowledge that you communicate, you have opened to him a vast field of the unknown and the wonderful. Thus it ever was and ever will be with the human mind; everything which it knows introduces to its observation a greater multitude of things which it does not know; the clearing up of one mystery conducts it to another; all its discoveries are bounded by a circle of doubt and ignorance which is wide in proportion to the knowledge it enfolds. It is a pledge of the immortal destinies of the human intellect that it is forever drawn by a strong attraction to the darker edge of this circle, and forever attempting to penetrate the obscurities beyond. The old world, then, is welcome to its mysteries; we need not envy it on that account: for, in addition to our superior knowledge and as a consequence of it, we have even more of them than it, and they are loftier, deeper, and more spiritual.

But the mythologies of antiquity!–in particular, the beautiful mythologies of Greece and Rome, of which so much enters into the charming remains of ancient poetry! Beautiful those mythologies unquestionably were, and exceedingly varied and delightfully adapted to many of the purposes of poetry; yet it may be doubted whether, on the whole, the art gained more by them than it lost. For remark that, so far as mystery is a quality of poetry, it has been taken away almost entirely by the myth. The fault of the myth was that it accounted for everything. It had a god for every operation of nature–a Jupiter to distil the showers and roll the thunder, a Phoebus to guide the chariot of the sun, a divinity to breathe the winds, a divinity to pour out every fountain. It left nothing in obscurity; everything was seen. Its very beauty consisted in minute disclosures. Thus the imagination was delighted, but neither the imagination nor the feelings were stirred up from their utmost depths. That system gave us the story of a superior and celestial race of beings, to whom human passions were attributed, and who were, like ourselves, susceptible of suffering; but it elevated them so far above the creatures of earth in power, in knowledge, and in security from the calamities of our condition, that they could be the subjects of little sympathy. Therefore it is that the mythological poetry of the ancients is as cold as it is beautiful, as unaffecting as it is faultless. And the genius of this mythological poetry, carried into the literature of a later age, where it was cultivated with a less sincere and earnest spirit, has been the destruction of all nature and simplicity. Men forsook the sure guidance of their own feelings and impressions, and fell into gross offences against taste. They wished to describe the passion of love, and they talked of Venus and her boy Cupid and his bow; they would speak of the freshness and glory of morning, and they fell to prattling of Phoebus and his steeds. No wonder that poetry has been thought a trifling art when thus practiced. For my part I cannot but think that human beings, placed among the things of this earth, with their affections and sympathies, their joys and sorrow, and the accidents of fortune to which they are liable, are infinitely a better subject for poetry than any imaginary race of creatures whatever. Let the fountain tell me of the flocks that have drunk at it; of the village girl that has gathered spring flowers on its margin; the traveller that has slaked his thirst there in the hot noon, and blessed its waters; the schoolboy that has pulled the nuts from the hazels that hang over it as it leaps and sparkles in its cool basin; let it speak of youth and health and purity and gladness, and I care not for the naiad that pours it out. If it must have a religious association, let it murmur of the invisible goodness that fills and feeds its reservoirs in the darkness of the earth. The admirers of poetry, then, may give up the ancient mythology without a sigh. Its departure has left us what is better than all it has taken away: it has left us men and women; it has left us the creatures and things of God's universe, to the simple charm of which the cold splendor of that system blinded men's eyes, and to the magnificence of which the rapid progress of science is every day adding new wonders and glories. It has left us, also, a more sublime and affecting religion, whose truths are broader, higher, nobler than any outlook to which its random conjectures ever attained.

With respect to later superstitions, traces of which linger yet in many districts of the civilized world–such as the belief in witchcraft, astrology, the agency of foul spirits in the affairs of men, in ghosts, fairies, water-sprites, and goblins of the wood and the mine–I would observe that the ages which gave birth to this fantastic brood are not those which have produced the noblest specimens of poetry. Their rise supposes a state of society too rude for the successful cultivation of the art. Nor does it seem to me that the bigoted and implicit reception of them is at all favorable to the exercise of poetic talent. Poetry, it is true, sometimes produces a powerful effect by appealing to that innate love of the supernatural which lies at the bottom of every man's heart and mind, and which all are willing to indulge, some freely and some by stealth, but it does this for the most part by means of those superstitions which exist rather in tradition than in serious belief. It finds them more flexible and accommodating; it is able to mould them to its purposes, and at liberty to reject all that is offensive. Accordingly, we find that even the poets of superstitious ages have been fond of going back to the wonders and prodigies of elder days. Those who invented fictions for the age of chivalry, which one would be apt to think had marvels enough of its own, delighted to astonish their readers with tales of giants, dragons, hippogriffs, and enchanters, the home of which was laid in distant ages, or, at least, in remote countries. The best witch ballad—with the exception, perhaps, of "Tam o' Shanter"—that I know of is Hogg's "Witch of Fife," yet both these were written long after the belief in witches had been laughed out of countenance.

It is especially the privilege of an age which has no engrossing superstitions of its own, to make use in its poetry of those of past ages; to levy contributions from the credulity of all time, and thus to diversify indefinitely the situations in which its human agents are placed. If these materials are managed with sufficient skill to win the temporary assent of the reader to the probability of the supernatural circumstances related, the purpose of the poet is answered. This is precisely the condition of the present age; it has the advantage over all ages that have preceded it in the abundance of those collected materials, and its poets have not been slow to avail themselves of their aid.

In regard to the circumstances which are thought in the present age to repress and limit the exercise of the poetical faculty, the principal if not the only one is supposed to be the prevalence of studies and pursuits unfavorable to the cultivation of the imagination and to enthusiasm of feeling. True it is that there are studies and pursuits which principally call into exercise other faculties of the mind, and that they are competitors with Poetry for the favor of the public. But it is not certain that the patronage bestowed on them would be extended to her, even if they should cease to exist. Nay, there is strong reason to suppose that they have done something to extend her influence, for they have certainly multiplied the number of readers, and everybody who reads at all sometimes reads poetry, and generally professes to admire what the best judges pronounce excellent, and, perhaps, in time come to enjoy it. Various inclinations continue, as heretofore, to impel one individual to one pursuit, and another to another—one to chemistry and another to poetry—yet I cannot see that their different labors interfere with each other, or that, because the chemist prosecutes his science successfully, therefore the poet should lose his inspiration. Take the example of Great Britain. In no country are the sciences studied with greater success, yet in no country is poetry pursued with more ardor. Spring and autumn reign hand in hand in her literature; it is loaded at once with blossoms and fruits. Does the poetry of that island of the present day—the poetry of Wordsworth, Scott, Coleridge, Byron, Southey, Shelley, and others— smack of the chilling tendencies of the physical sciences? Or, rather, is it not bold, varied, impassioned, irregular, and impatient of precise laws, beyond that of any former age? Indeed, has it not the freshness, the vigor, and perhaps also the disorder, of a new literature?

The amount of knowledge necessary to be possessed by all who would keep pace with the age, as much greater as it is than formerly, is not, I apprehend, in danger of oppressing and smothering poetical talent. Knowledge is the material with which Genius builds her fabrics. The greater its abundance, the more power is required to dispose it into order and beauty, but the more vast and magnificent will be the structure. All great poets have been men of great knowledge. Some have gathered it from books, as Spenser and Milton; others from keen observation of men and things, as Homer and Shakespeare. On the other hand, the poetry of Ossian, whether genuine or not, is an instance of no inconsiderable poetical talent struggling with the disadvantages of a want of knowledge. It is this want which renders it so singularly monotonous. The poverty of the poet's ideas confined his mind to a narrow circle, and his poems are a series of changes rung upon a few thoughts and a few images. Single passages are beautiful and affecting, but each poem, as a whole, is tiresome and uninteresting.

I come, in the last place, to consider the question of our own expectations in literature, and the probability of our producing in the new world anything to rival the immortal poems of the old. Many of the remarks already made on the literary spirit of the present age will apply also to this part of the subject. Indeed, in this point of view, we should do ill to despair of our country, at least until the lapse of many years shall seem to have settled the question against us. Where the fountains of knowledge are by the roadside, and where the volumes from which poetic enthusiasms are caught and fed are in everybody's hands, it would be singularly strange if amid the multitude of pursuits which occupy our citizens, nobody should think of taking verse as a path to fame. Yet, if it shall be chosen and pursued with the characteristic ardor of our countrymen, what can prevent its being brought to the same degree of perfection here as in other countries? Not the want of encouragement surely, for the literary man needs but little to stimulate his exertions, and with that little his exertions are undoubtedly greater. Who would think of fattening a race-horse? Complaints of the poverty of poets are as old as their art, but I never heard that they wrote the worse verses for it. It is enough, probably, to call forth their most vigorous efforts, that poetry is admired and honored by their countrymen. With respect to the paucity of national traditions, it will be time to complain of it when all those of which we are possessed are exhausted. Besides, as I have already shown, it is the privilege of poets, when they suppose themselves in need of materials, to seek them in other countries. The best English poets have done this. The events of Spenser's celebrated poem take place within the shadowy limits of fairy-land. Shakespeare has laid the scene of many of his finest tragedies in foreign countries. Milton went out of the world for the subject of his two epics. Byron has taken the incidents of all his poems from outside of England. Southey's best work is a poem of Spain—of chivalry, and of the Roman Church. For the story of one of his narrative poems, Moore went to Persia; for that of another, to the antediluvian world. Wordsworth and Crabbe, each in a different way, and each with great power, abjuring all heroic traditions and recollections, and all aid from the supernatural and the marvellous, have drawn their subjects from modern manners and the simple occurrences of common life. Are they read, for that reason, with any the less avidity by the multitudes who resort to their pages for pastime, for edification, for solace, for noble joy, and for the ecstasies of pure delight?

It has been urged by some, as an obstacle to the growth of elegant literature among us, that our language is a transplanted one, framed for a country and for institutions different from ours, and, therefore, not likely to be wielded by us with such force, effect, and grace, as it would have been if it had grown up with our nation, and received its forms and its accessions from the exigences of our experience. It seems to me that this is one of the most unsubstantial of all the brood of phantoms which have been conjured up to alarm us. Let those who press this opinion descend to particulars. Let them point out the peculiar defects of our language in its application to our natural and political situation. Let them show in what respects it refuses to accommodate itself easily and gracefully to all the wants of expression that are felt among us. Till they do this, let us be satisfied that the copious and flexible dialect we speak is as equally proper to be used at the equator as at the poles, and at any intermediate latitude; and alike in monarchies or republics. It has grown up, as every forcible and beautiful language has done, among a simple and unlettered people; it has accommodated itself, in the first place, to the things of nature, and, as civilization advanced, to the things of art; and thus it has become a language full of picturesque forms of expression, yet fitted for the purposes of science. If a new language were to arise among us in our present condition of society, I fear that it would derive too many of its words from the roots used to signify canals, railroads, and steam-boats—things which, however well thought of at present, may perhaps a century hence be superseded by still more ingenious inventions. To try this notion about a transplanted dialect, imagine one of the great living poets of England emigrated to this country. Can anybody be simple enough to suppose that his poetry would be the worse for it?

I infer, then, that all the materials of poetry exist in our own country, with all the ordinary encouragements and opportunities for making a successful use of them. The elements of beauty and grandeur, intellectual greatness and moral truth, the stormy and the gentle passions, the casualties and the changes of life, and the light shed upon man's nature by the story of past times and the knowledge of foreign manners, have not made their sole abode in the old world beyond the waters. If under these circumstances our poetry should finally fail of rivalling that of Europe, it will be because Genius sits idle in the midst of its treasures.

America and Its Novel

REVIEW OF CATHARINE M. SEDGWICK'S *REDWOOD*

This is a story of domestic life, the portraiture of what passes by our firesides and in our streets, in the calm of the country, and amidst a prosperous and well ordered community. The writer, who, we understand, is the same lady to whom the public is already indebted for another beautiful little work of a similar character, has not availed herself of the more obvious and abundant sources of interest which would naturally suggest themselves to the author of a fictitious history, the scene of which should be laid in the United States. She has not gone back to the infancy of our country to try to set before us the fearless and hardy men who made the first lodgement in its vast forests, men in whose characters is to be found the favorite material of the novelist, great virtues mingled with many errors, the strange land to which they had come, and its unknown dangers, and the savage tribes by whom they were surrounded, to whose kindness they owed so much, and from whose enmity they suffered so severely. Nor does the thread of her narrative lead us through those early feuds between the different colonies of North America, who brought with them and kept alive, in their settlements, the animosities of the nations from whom they proceeded, and, in the midst of all their hardships and sufferings, contended about the division of the wilderness with a fierceness and an obstinacy exasperated by the difference in the characters of those who composed them. Nor has the writer made any use of the incidents of our great national struggle for independence, at once so calamitous and so glorious, the time of splendid virtues and great sufferings, the war which separated friends, and divided families, and revived the half laid spirit of bloodshed in the uncivilised races about us, and called to our shores so many military adventurers to fight under the standard of Britain, and so many generous volunteers in the cause of humanity and liberty to combat under ours. She has passed by all these periods and situations—so tempting to the writer of fictitious history, so pregnant with interest and teeming with adventure—to make a more hazardous experiment of her powers. She has come down to the very days in which we live, to quiet times and familiar manners, and has laid the scene of her narrative in the most ancient and tranquil parts of the country; presenting us not merely with the picture of what she has imagined, but with the copy of what she has observed.

We have called this a comparatively hazardous experiment–and this because it seems to us far more difficult to deal successfully with the materials which the author has chosen than with those which she has neglected. There is a strong love of romance inherent in the human mind. We all remember how our childhood was captivated with stories of sorcerers and giants. We do not, in out riper age, forget with what a fearful and thrilling interest we hung over·tales of the interpositions of supernatural beings, of acts of desperate heroism, followed by incredible successes, of impossible dangers, and equally impossible deliverances. And when our maturer judgment has caused us to turn with disgust from the relation of what is contrary to the known laws of nature, we transfer the same intense attention to narratives that keep within the bounds of possibility. We love to read of imminent perils and hair-breadth escapes, of adventures in strange lands and among strange races of men, or in times of great public commotion or unusual public calamity. Something of this taste exists in every mind, though variously modified and diversified, and contented with a greater or less degree of verisimilitude, according as the imagination is more or less inflammable. Some preserve a fondness for fictions almost as wild as those which amused their earlier years, while others can be pleased only with the recital of what is strictly probable. Some will listen with interest to stories of "antres vast and deserts idle," and the adventures of the intrepid voyager who traverses them, while others delight to have their blood curdle at being told of

> The Anthropophagi, and men whose heads
> Do grow beneath their shoulders.

in reading narratives of the romantic kind, our curiosity comes in aid of the author. We are eager to learn the issue of adventures so new to us. The imagination of the reader is also ready with its favorable offices. This faculty, always busiest when we are told of scenes and events out of the range of men's ordinary experience, expatiates at large upon the suggestions of the author, and, as we read, rapidly fills up the outline he gives with bright colors and deep shades of its own. From all these causes it may happen that, by the mere fortunate invention and happy arrangement of striking incidents, a work of fiction shall succeed in gaining the public favor, without any considerable proportion of the higher merits of that kind of writing, without any uncommon beauty of style, or any unusual degree either of pathos or humor, or splendor of imagination, or vivacity of description, or powerful delineation of character.

But with a novel founded on domestic incidents, supposed to happen in our own time and country, the case is different. We have seen the original, and require that there be no false coloring or distortion in the copy. We want to be delighted with the development of traits that had escaped our observation, or of which, if observed, we had never felt the peculiar significance. It will not do to trust to the imagination of the reader to heighten the interest of such a narrative; if it ever attempts to fill up the sketch given by the writer, it is not often in a way calculated to increase its effect, for it is done with the plain and sober hues that color the tissue of our own lives. We are too familiar with the sort of life described, we are too well acquainted with the situation in which the characters are placed, we have stood too long in the very relations out of which grows the interest of the narrative, to be much interested by reading about them, unless they are vividly and strikingly set before us. These are things which have so often moved the heart in their reality that it refuses to be strongly affected by them in a fictitious narrative, unless they are brought home to it and pressed upon it with more than ordinary power. They are chords that will not yield their music to the passing wind; they must be touched by the hand of a master. The mere description of ordinary, everyday scenes and events is too plain a banquet to be relished without some condiment to make it palatable. Readers require not only the exclusion of those tame scenes and incidents, without connexion or consequence., that make up so much of real life, but that the incidents set down be related with pathos, or at least with spirit or humor they look for natural and sprightly dialogue, and well drawn characters.

On more than one occasion, we have already given somewhat at large our opinion of the fertility of our country, and its history, in the materials of romance. If our reasonings needed any support from successful examples of that kind of writing, as a single fact is worth a volume of ingenious theorising, we have had the triumph of seeing them confirmed beyond all controversy by the works of a popular American author who has shown the literary world into what beautiful creations those materials may be wrought. In like manner, we look upon the specimen before us as a conclusive argument that the writers of works of fiction, of which the scene is laid in familiar and domestic life, have a rich and varied field before them in the United States. Indeed, the opinion on this subject–which, till lately, prevailed pretty extensively among us–that works of this kind, descriptive of the manners of our countrymen, could not succeed, never seemed to us to rest on a very solid foundation. It was rather a sweeping inference drawn from the fact that no highly meritorious work of the kind had appeared, and the most satisfactory and comfortable way of accounting for this was to assert that no such could be written. But it is not always safe to predict what a writer of genius will make of any given subject. Twenty years ago, what possible conception could an English critic have had of the admirable productions of the author of *Waverley*, and of the wonderful improvement of his example has effected in that kind of composition? Had the idea of one of those captivating works, destined to take such strong hold on all minds, been laid before him by the future author, he would probably only have wondered at his vanity.

There is nothing paradoxical in the opinion which maintains that all civilised countries–we had almost said all countries whatever– furnish matter for copies of real life, embodied in works of fiction, which shall be of lasting and general interest. Wherever there are human nature and society, there are subjects for the novelist. The passions and affections, virtue and vice, are of no country. Everywhere love comes to touch the hearts of the young, and everywhere scorn and jealousy, the obstacles of fortune and the prudence of the aged, are at hand to disturb the course of love. Everywhere there exists the desire of wealth, the love of power, and the wish to be admired, courage braving real dangers, and cowardice shrinking from imaginary ones, friendship and hatred, and all the train of motives and impulses which affect the minds and influence the conduct of men. They not only exist everywhere, but they exist infinitely diversified and compounded, in various degrees of suppression and restraint, or fostered into unnatural growth and activity, modified by political institutions and laws, by national religions and subdivisions of those religions, by different degrees of refinement and civilisation, of poverty or of abundance, by arbitrary usages handed down from indefinite antiquity, and even by local situation and climate. Nor is there a single one of all these innumerable modifications of human character and human emotion which is not, in some degree, an object of curiosity and interest. Over all the world is human sagacity laying its plans, and chance and the malice of others are thwarting them, and fortune is raising up one man and throwing down another. In none of the places of human habitation are the accesses barred against joy or grief; the kindness of the good carries gladness into families, and the treachery of the false friend brings sorrow and ruin; in all countries are tears shed over the graves of the excellent, the brave, and the beautiful, and the oppressed breathe freer when the oppressor has gone to his account. Everywhere has nature her features of grandeur and of beauty, and these features receive a moral expression from the remembrances of the past, and the interests or the present. On her face, as on an immense theatre, the passions and pursuits of men are performing the great drama of human existence. At every moment, and in every corner of the world, these mighty and restless agents are perpetually busy, under an infinity of forms and disguises, and the great representation goes on with that majestic continuity and uninterrupted regularity which mark all the courses of nature. Who then will undertake to say that the hand of genius may not pencil off a few scenes, acted in our own vast country, and amidst our large population, that shall interest and delight the world?

It is a native writer only that must or can do this. It is he that must show how the infinite diversities of human character are yet further varied, by causes that exist in our own country, exhibit our peculiar modes of thinking and action, and mark the effect of these upon individual fortunes and happiness. A foreigner is manifestly incompetent to the task; his observation would rest only upon the more general and obvious traits of our national character; a thousand delicate shades of manner would escape his notice, many interesting peculiarities would never come to his knowledge, and many more he would misapprehend. It is only on his native soil that the author of such works can feel himself on safe and firm ground, that he can move confidently and fearlessly, and put forth the whole strength of his powers without risk of failure. His delineations of character and action, if executed with ability, will have a raciness and freshness about them which will attest their fidelity, the secret charm which belongs to truth and nature, and with which even the finest genius cannot invest a system of adscititious and imaginary manners. It is this quality which recommends them powerfully to the sympathy and interest even of those, who are unacquainted with the original from which they are drawn, and makes such pictures from such hands so delightful and captivating to the foreigner. By super-adding, to the novelty of the manners described, the interest of a narrative, they create a sort of illusion which places him in the midst of the country where the action of the piece is going on. He beholds the scenery of a distant land, hears its inhabitants conversing about their own concerns in their own dialect, finds himself in the bosom of its families, is made the depository of their secrets and the observer of their fortunes, and becomes an inmate of their firesides without stirring from his own. Thus it is that American novels are eagerly read in Great Britain, and novels descriptive of English and Scottish manners as eagerly read in America.

It has been objected that the habits of our countrymen are too active and practical; that they are too universally and continually engrossed by the cares and occupations of business to have leisure for that intrigue, those plottings and counter plottings which are necessary to give a sufficient degree of action and eventfulness to the novel of real life. It is said that we need for this purpose a class of men whose condition in life places them above the necessity of active exertion, and who are driven to the practice of intrigue because they have nothing else to do. It remains, however, to be proved that any considerable portion of this ingredient is necessary in the composition of a successful novel. To require that it should be made up of nothing better than the manoeuvres of those whose only employment is to glitter at places of public resort, to follow a perpetual round of amusements, and to form plans to outshine, thwart, and vex each other, is confining the writer to a narrow and most barren circle. It is requiring an undue proportion of heartlessness, selfishness, and vice in his pictures of society. It is compelling him to go out of the wholesome atmosphere of those classes, where the passions and affections have their most salutary and natural play, and employ his observations on that where they are most perverted, sophisticated, and corrupt. But will it be seriously contended that he can have no other resource but the rivalries and machinations of the idle, the frivolous, and the dissolute to keep the reader from yawning over his pictures? Will it be urged that no striking and interesting incidents can come to pass without their miserable aid? If our country be not the country of intrigue, it is at least the country of enterprise; and nowhere are the great objects that worthily interest the passions, and call forth the exertions of men, pursued with more devotion and perseverance. The agency of chance too is not confined to the shores of Europe; our countrymen have not attained a sufficient degree of certainty in their calculations to exclude it from ours. It would really seem to us that these two sources, along with that proportion of the blessed quality of intrigue which even the least favorable view of our society will allow us, are abundantly fertile in interesting occurrences for all the purposes of the novelist. Besides, it should be recollected, that it is not in any case the dull diary of ordinary occupations, or amusements, that forms the groundwork of his plot. On the contrary, it is some event, or at least a series of events, of unusual importance, standing out in strong relief from the rest of the biography of his principal characters, and to which the daily habits of their lives, whatever may be their rank or condition, are only a kind of accompaniment.

But the truth is that the distinctions of rank, and the amusements of elegant idleness, are but the surface of society, and only so many splendid disguises put upon the reality of things. They are trappings which the writer of real genius, the anatomist of the human heart, strips away when he would exhibit his characters as they are, and engage our interest for them as beings of our own species. He reduces them to the same great level where distinctions of rank are nothing, and difference of character everything. It is here that James First, and Charles Second, and Louis Ninth, and Rob Roy, and Jeanie Deans, and Meg Merrilies are, by the great author of the Waverley Novels, made to meet. The monarch must come down from the dim elevation of his throne; he must lay aside the assumed and conventional manners of his station, and unbend and unbosom himself with his confidants, before that illustrious master will condescend to describe him. In the artificial sphere in which the great move, they are only puppets and pageants, but here they are men. A narrative, the scene of which is laid at the magnificent levees of princes, in the drawing rooms of nobles, and the bright assemblies of fashion, may be a very pretty, showy sort of thing, and so may a story of the glittering dances and pranks of fairies. But we soon grow weary of all this, and ask for objects of sympathy and regard, for something the recollection of which shall dwell on the heart, and to which it will love to recur; for something, in short, which is natural, the uneffaced traits of strength and weakness, of the tender and the comic, all which the pride of rank either removes from observation or obliterates.

If these things have any value, we hesitate not to say that they are to be found abundantly in the characters of our countrymen, formed as they are under the influence of our free institutions, and shooting into a large and vigorous, though sometimes irregular luxuriance. They exist most abundantly in our more ancient settlements, and amidst the more homogeneous races of our large populations, where the causes that produce them have operated longest and with most activity. It is there that the human mind has learned best to enjoy our fortunate and equal institutions, and to profit by them. In the countries of Europe the laws chain men down to the condition in which they were burn. This observation, of course, is not equally true of all those countries, but when they are brought into comparison with ours, it is in some degree applicable to them all. Men spring up, and vegetate, and die without thinking of passing from the sphere in which they find themselves any more than the plants they cultivate think of removing from the places where they are rooted. It is the tendency of this rigid and melancholy destiny to contract and stint the intellectual faculties, to prevent the development of character, and to make the subjects of it timid, irresolute, and imbecile. With us, on the contrary, where the proudest honors in the state and the highest deference in society are set equally before all our citizens, a wholesome and quickening impulse is communicated to all parts of the social system. All are possessed with a spirit of ambition and a love of adventure, an intense competition calls forth and exalts the passions and faculties of men, their characters become strongly defined, their minds acquire a hardihood and activity which can be gained by no other discipline, and the community, throughout all its conditions, is full of bustle, and change, and action.

Whoever will take the pains to pursue this subject a little into its particulars will be surprised at the infinite variety of forms of character which spring up under the institutions of our country. Religion is admitted on all hands to be a mighty agent in moulding the human character; and accordingly, with the perfect allowance and toleration of all religions, we see among us their innumerable and diverse influences upon the manners and temper of our people. Whatever may be his religious opinions, no one is restrained by fear of consequences from avowing them, but is left to nurse his peculiarities of doctrine into what importance he pleases. The Quaker is absolved from submission to the laws in those particulars which offend his conscience, the Moravian finds no barriers in the way of his work of proselytism and charity, the Roman Catholic is subjected to no penalty for pleasing himself with the magnificent ceremonial of his religion, and the Jew worships unmolested in his synagogue. In many parts of our country we see communities of that strange denomination, the Shakers, distinguished from their neighbors by a garb, a dialect, an architecture, a way of worship, of thinking, and of living, as different as if they were in fact of a different origin, instead of being collected from the families around them. In other parts we see small neighborhoods of the Seventh Day Baptists, retaining the simplicity of manners and quaintness of language delivered down from their fathers. Here we find the austerities of puritanism preserved to this day, there the rights and doctrines of the Church of England are shown in their effect on the manners of the people, and yet in another part of the country springs up a new and numerous sect, who wash one another's feet and profess to revive the primitive habits of the apostolic times.

It is in our country also that these differences of character, which grow naturally out of geographical situation, are least tampered with and repressed by political regulations. The adventurous and roving natives of our seacoast and islands are a different race of men from those who till the interior, and the hardy dwellers of our mountainous districts are not like the inhabitants of the rich plains that skirt our mighty lakes and rivers. The manners of the northern states are said to be characterised by the keenness and importunity of their climate, and those of the southern to partake of the softness of theirs. In our cities you will see the polished manners of the European capitals, but pass into the more quiet and unvisited parts of the country, and you will find men whom you might take for the first planters of our colonies. The descendants of the Hollanders have not forgotten the traditions of their fathers, and the legends of Germany are still recited, and the ballads of Scotland still sung, in settlements whose inhabitants derive their origin from those countries. It is hardly possible that the rapid and continual growth and improvement of our country, a circumstance wonderfully exciting to the imagination, and altogether unlike anything witnessed in other countries, should not have some influence in forming our national character. At all events, it is a most fertile source of incident. It does for us in a few short years what, in Europe, is the work of centuries. The hardy and sagacious native of the eastern states settles himself in the wilderness by the side of the emigrant from British Isles; the pestilence of the marshes is braved and overcome; the bear, and wolf and catamount are chased from their haunts; and then you see cornfields and roads and towns springing up as if by enchantment. In the mean time pleasant Indian villages, situated on the skirts of their hunting grounds, with their beautiful green plats for dances and martial exercises, are taken into the bosom of our extending population, while new states are settled and cities founded far beyond them. Thus a great deal of history is crowded into a brief space. Each little hamlet, in a few seasons, has more events and changes to tell of than a European village can furnish in a course of ages.

But, if the writer of fictitious history does not find all the variety he wishes in the various kinds of our population–descended, in different parts of our country, from ancestors of different nations, and yet preserving innumerable and indubitable tokens of their origin–, if the freedom with which every man is suffered to take his own way, in all things not affecting the peace and good order of society, does not furnish him with a sufficient diversity of characters, employments, and modes of life, he has yet other resources. He may bring into his plots men whose characters and manners were formed by the institutions and modes of society in the nations beyond the Atlantic, and he may describe them faithfully as things which he has observed and studied. If he is not satisfied with indigenous virtue, he may take for the model of his characters men of whom the old world is not worthy, and whom it has cast out from its bosom. If domestic villany be not dark enough for his pictures, here are fugitives from the justice of Europe come to prowl in America. If the coxcombs of our own country are not sufficiently exquisite, affected, and absurd, here are plenty of silken fops from the capitals of foreign kingdoms. If he finds himself in need of a class of men more stupid and degraded than are to be found among the natives of the United States, here are crowds of the wretched peasantry of Great Britain and Germany, flying for refuge from intolerable suffering, in every vessel that comes to our shores. Hither also resort numbers of that order of men who, in foreign countries, are called the middling class, the most valuable part of the communities they leave, to enjoy a moderate affluence, where the abuses and exactions of a distempered system of government cannot reach them, to degrade them to the condition of the peasantry. Our country is the asylum of the persecuted preachers of new religions, and the teachers of political doctrines, which Europe will not endure; a sanctuary for dethroned princes, and the consorts of slain emperors. When we consider all these innumerable differences of character, native and foreign, this infinite variety of pursuits and objects, this endless diversity and change of fortunes, and behold them gathered and grouped into one vast assemblage in our own country, we shall feel little pride in the sagacity or the skill of that native author who asks for a richer or a wider field of observation.

* * *

The peculiarities in the manners and character of our countrymen have too long been connected with ideas merely low and ludicrous. We complain of our English neighbors for holding them up as objects simply ridiculous and laughable, but it is by no means certain that we have not encouraged them by our example. It is time, however, that they were redeemed from these gross and degrading associations. It is time that they should be mentioned, as they deserve to be, with something else than a sneer, and that a feeling of respect should mingle with the smile they occasion. We are happy to see the author of this work connecting them, as we find them connected in real life, with much that is ennobling and elevated, with traits of sagacity, benevolence, moral courage and magnanimity. These are qualities which by no means impair any comic effect those peculiarities may have; they rather relieve and heighten it. They transform it from mere buffoonery to the finest humor. When this is done, something is done to exalt our national reputation abroad, and to improve our national character at home. It is also a sort of public benefit to show what copious and valuable materials the private lives and daily habits of our countrymen offer to the writer of genius. It is as if one were to discover to us rich ores and gems lying in the common earth about us. But our readers must by this time be weary of our comments, and we dismiss them, with pleasure, to the perusal of the work itself.

Commentary, by Frank Gado

Reconsiderations

The Founding Father of American Poetry

Contrary to claims often lodged for various poets from the colonial period through the first decades of the early republic, our nation's poetic tradition is moored to the 1821 publication of William Cullen Bryant's *Poems*. To be sure, unlike James Fenimore Cooper's *The Spy*, issued that same year, or Washington Irving's *The Sketch Book* a year earlier–resounding successes that first alerted large audiences on both sides of the Atlantic that American fiction was coming of age–this slim volume of verse attracted few purchasers. Indeed, Bryant had previously won far greater renown as the thirteen-year-old author of *The Embargo*, a harsh attack on President Jefferson that had sold so well in 1808 it quickly warranted a second, expanded edition. But that flurry of interest had arisen from political motives, combined with astonishment at its author's precocity. Bryant himself soon wished the brash couplets forgotten, and once Madison replaced Jefferson in the White House, the public obliged him. *Poems* was an achievement of a quite different order. Even though its few critical notices were regional, unsophisticated, and discerned nothing of particular import, *Poems* set in motion the acceptance of Bryant as America's poet and of his poetry as America's natural voice.

The collection's origin traced to a handful of fragments Dr. Peter Bryant snatched from his son's desk in 1817 and passed on to Willard Phillips, a literary friend affiliated with the *North American Review*. These verses soon appeared in the magazine–though spliced by mistake and erroneously attributed, in part, to the father. Bryant's next submissions continued to impress; the editors even dared believe they had chanced on the nation's rising great poet. Yet publication in the *North American*, for all of that periodical's lofty sense of itself, could not make a reputation. Although Americans were spawning magazines at an accelerating rate, few survived long enough to wield palpable influence or to develop an audience beyond their home territory. In addition, Bryant's entrance into the *North American* occurred at a moment when the editorial board was riven over whether the magazine should continue to publish poetry. Clearly, if Bryant was to win recognition as his generation's preeminent poet, he would require another, more resonant instrument. Harvard College, with its close ties to the *North American*, was an obvious choice.

Evidently at the urging of Phillips, of Edward Channing (a faculty member formerly the magazine's editor), and of Richard Henry Dana (who saw himself as champion of America's "new poetry"), the college's Phi Beta Kappa Society invited Bryant to speak at the 1821 commencement. Some risk attended the bid, for none of his promoters had yet met this young benedict who had been reining in his literary ambitions while striving to build a law practice in the Western Massachusetts hinterland. Presumably for this reason, the Society's secretary made a point of advising him to take pains with his oral delivery so as to win the distinguished Cambridge audience's favor. More significantly, the Society also counseled him to select American literature as his subject.[*]

This was far from a casual suggestion. Bryant had already shown his mettle as a scholar and critic: in reviewing Solyman Brown's book on American poetry for the *North American* in 1818, he had summarily dismissed the author as incompetent, then supplied his own astute assessments in a pioneering survey–perhaps the first overview of the nation's poets worth any heed. Three years later, with American writing at last starting to gain respect, he found himself advantageously situated to capitalize on the new spirit of literary nationalism. The most obvious ploy would have been to use his scholarly platform to issue a manifesto, implicitly nominating himself to usher in the future. But Bryant chose another course. Instead of describing America's literary promise, he devoted the summer to producing a poem which would exemplify it.

Four decades earlier, political independence had immediately mandated a view of the new nation as the creature of history, working to accomplish a divinely appointed destiny. Literary independence was soon coupled to expression of that unique role: being a major American poet entailed bardic celebration of the nation's founding as the climax

---

[*]Apparently, the Phi Beta Kappa Society had a standing interest in the emergence of an American literature. Addressing the Society in 1809, the Reverend J.S. Buckminster had appraised the nation's literary product and found it sterile. Greatness was entirely prospective, he declared; yet, straining to be hopeful, he found signs of our genius "meditat[ing] a bolder flight," so that "the generation which is to succeed us will be formed on better models and leave a brighter track."

of Western civilization. Joel Barlow had self-consciously taken on the task–first in *The Vision of Columbus*, then in *The Columbiad*–as had Phillip Freneau, collaborating with Hugh Henry Brackenridge in "The Rising Glory of America" (also written for a college commencement). Bryant himself, when he was barely fifteen, had tried his hand at the subject in "The Genius of Columbia." Now, at the age of twenty-six, he had earned enough credibility with his small body of highly regarded work to warrant return to this epic theme as a poet worthy of it. The summons to Cambridge, capped by declamation of a grand national poem before the august assembly, bore comparison to a rite of investiture.[*]

In the event, the opportunity for a triumph went unrealized. A temperate man, Bryant gave a subdued performance; his manner ill-suited the period's oratorical tastes, and no newspaper judged it worth more than simple mention in the account of the ceremony's program. Even so, the recitation fully met his sponsors' purpose. Before Bryant left Boston, he arranged for the printing of *Poems*, just as they had planned. "The Ages," the poem he composed for the Phi Beta Kappa presentation, led the volume.

That placing could not have been more telling: in effect, the poem serves as a standard unfurled by the nation's poet, whose role is to demonstrate that America expresses a divine plan. Eight stanzas

---

[*]Among those present was Secretary of State James Quincy Adams, whom Bryant had pilloried in "The Embargo" fourteen years earlier. Others–in addition to most of the *North American* cohort: Phillips, Edward and William Ellery Channing, Richard Henry Dana, and Washington Allston–included former Secretary of State Timothy Pickering, Congressman (soon to be mayor of Boston, then Harvard president) Josiah Quincy, and Edward Everett (recently appointed Professor of Greek at Harvard but already well on the way toward recognition as the nation's foremost orator).

Ralph Waldo Emerson, graduating from Harvard that year, presumably heard Bryant read his poem. (Letters of introduction from Emerson imply he had met Bryant during the commencement exercises.) Sixteen years and a day later, Emerson would also address the Phi Beta Kappa Society. By then the subject urged upon Bryant had become the Society's annual assigned topic; subsequently known as "The American Scholar," Emerson's oration is often cited as America's Declaration of Intellectual Independence. The nationalistic hurrah linking the two writers resounds from Emerson's introductory paragraph: "Events, actions arise [in America], that must be sung, that will sing themselves. Who can doubt, that poetry will revive and lead in a new age, as the star in the constellation Harp ... , astronomers announce, shall one day be the pole star for a thousand years."

introduce a twenty- seven scene historical pageant–from Cain's slaying of Abel to American Independence–designed to portray, in Bryant's words, "the successive advances of mankind in knowledge, virtue, and happiness, to justify and confirm the hopes of the philanthropist for the future destinies of mankind." Such callow chauvinism may embarrass the modern reader, but at the time "The Ages" was written the concept was a commonplace. To claim importance as a poet was necessarily to publish an epic–or, at the very least, to employ an epic treatment of the American past and future. Over the preceding four decades, many dozens of patriotic poems in newspapers and magazines proclaimed that American history confirmed destiny. (Even past the middle of the nineteenth century, Walt Whitman would illustrate that being a self-conscious "poet of America" meant extolling the American example in democracy's spread throughout the world.) For the rest of Bryant's life, "Author of 'The Ages' " would appear on the title pages of his books–an advertisement, as it were, of his office as the country's unappointed poet laureate–and the poem itself would continue to occupy the first position in all his subsequent poetry collections.

Yet despite such emphasis, as well as a rather sturdy reputation as one of the major American poems for much of the nineteenth century, "The Ages" ranks at the lowest levels of Bryant's works. Its grandiosity dooms it. In pressing an epic intention, it reduces history to a rush of flash cards, one stanza per card, and its generally naïve pronouncements are disingenuously tailored to lend force to its patriotic affect.[*] A sense of elevated purpose also dictated the choice of Spenserian

---

*After the New World enters the chronicle with the description of a paradisaic Indian hamlet, innocence yields to bloody wars–waged, not by Europeans, but by other Indian tribes. When the white settlers arrive, the natives have exterminated themselves, thereby expediting the rise of Protestant industry and civic virtue, crowned by formation of the United States:

> Look now abroad–another race has filled
> These populous borders–wide the wood recedes,
> And towns shoot up, and fertile realms are tilled;
> The land is full of harvests and green meads;
>
> Here the free spirit of mankind, at length,
> Throws its last fetters off; and who shall place
> A limit to the giant's unchained strength,
> Or curb his swiftness in the forward race?

stanzas, a form the eighteenth century had deemed appropriate for subjects of moment and gravity. Given Bryant's keen interest at the time in exploring new possibilities beyond the straits of poetic convention, this reversion to a standard protocol can only have impeded his creative energies. The central reason the poem generates so little power, however, is that its subject does not suit its author's gifts.

Later, as editor and then owner of New York's *Evening Post*, Bryant boldly embraced democratic principles and liberal positions on most issues at home and abroad, but this enthusiasm mainly steered his journalism. Relatively few poems address political themes, and none is among his better efforts. For all his emphasis on establishing himself as the national bard, "The Ages" is nearly as false an indicator of his future poetic significance as "The Embargo." The true signpost of his genius rises from the volume's other half dozen poems: "To a Waterfowl," "Inscription for the Entrance to a Wood," "The Yellow Violet," "Song" (subsequently retitled "The Hunter of the West"), "Green River," and the completed version of "Thanatopsis" (an eighth poem, quite different and possibly the earliest written, was a translated fragment from Simonides).

Earlier American poets had chosen topics from nature, and British practice in the later decades of the eighteenth century was already making blank verse the fashion for meditations stimulated by natural observations; even so, *Poems* unveiled a new kind of poet, summed up in the sobriquet he soon acquired: "the American Wordsworth." The identification was rather facile: as a careful and eager student of his craft, Bryant owed debts to many predecessors. Like most young poets of his time, he had briefly been swept up in the Byron phenomenon, and, as he often acknowledged, he also learned from Mark Akenside, William Cowper, James Thomson, Edward Young, and Robert Burns—among others. But for all its over-simplification, the association with the chief revolutionary of English Romantic poetry properly assigned Bryant to the surge of the future instead of to the forms and sensibilities of the receding eighteenth century. The Romantic poet did not merely advocate a new mode of writing; he manifested a different understanding of the world, of the human relationship to that physical universe, and of art as the mediating element. Bryant registered the literary and philosophical changes that were in process, but what has not been sufficiently recognized is that he was also an authentic innovator.

"On the Use of Trisyllabic Feet in Iambic Verse," an essay Bryant began writing at sixteen (or possibly even earlier), seems quite unexceptionable today; in the history of poetic taste and its author's own evolution, however, it signaled a pivotal moment. Alexander Pope had died in 1744, yet his precise, regular verse persisted as the model for poets well towards the close of the century, and in America, fealty to his authority allowed almost no exception. Bryant himself had been trained in Pope's tradition by his father, and the master of Twickenham remained the son's paragon until he began preparing for Williams College. With that immersion in the classical poets came an awareness that Greek and Latin models set a false standard for English, and he understood that variety in the service of sense and sound rescued poetry from monotony. "Trisyllabic Feet" treats what may seem a trivial matter–the insertion of an extra syllable in a foot of iambic meter–but its implications are not at all trivial.

Bryant's attack targets the slavish adherence to metric rigidity then accepted as a criterion; to win his case he presents a brief, showing that the best poets have deviated from iambic regularity, not in occasional, incidental, and excusable lapses but in "agreeable" adherence "to the habits of our language." Initially, he focuses on blank verse and, par excellence, cites "the sweetest passages of Shakespeare–those which appear to have been struck out in the ecstasy of genius, and flow with that natural melody which is peculiar to him." That melodic element, he continues, is what makes blank verse poetry. But Bryant is not content to rest with that assertion. The same argument must also apply in rhymed verse, he reasons, because there is nothing inherent in rhyme that would compensate for the absence of melody. In this respect, Bryant ventures well beyond Wordsworth's call in his "advertisement" to the Lyrical Ballads for a "language of conversation" in poetry. Wordsworth, writing about ordinary people and ordinary activities, insisted on a corresponding diction, but he stopped far short of considering the natural interplay between tonality and cadence in a new approach to meter. Bryant's essay, however, clearly steers in that direction. Even in discerning the rules by which poets in the past elided syllables in order to fit exactly into a metrical scheme, Bryant pays particular attention to how sound affects the possibilities. And in defending the license to write an iambic line with an extra syllable or two, he is less interested in breaking down conventions than he is in giving precedence to the voice. Wordsworth claimed he sought to write poetry that was metered prose. Bryant proposes a more intricate feat: pursuit of the "uniquely poetic" through complex sonant relationships among clusters of meaning. "Trisyllabic Feet" is not itself a manifesto detailing a new aesthetic prescription, but in urging the removal of artificial, unnecessary restraints, a young American poet who had barely begun to be noticed was challenging the conventional discipline of his time:

The liberty for which I have been contending, has often been censured and ridiculed. The utmost favour which it has, at any time, to my knowledge, received from critics, is to have been silently allowed–no one has openly defended it. It has not been my aim to mark its limits or to look for its rules. I have only attempted to show that it is an ancient birthright of the poets, and it ought not to be given up.

More than Bryant's scholarly analysis of past practices, however, it is his poetry that demonstrates his reforming concepts of meter. In 1811, he was testing ideas about prosody that would intrigue Gerard Manley Hopkins three-quarters of a century later–and that, when Robert Bridges printed Hopkins's work posthumously in 1918, would both puzzle poets and pique their curiosity. Hopkins would dub his "discovery" *sprung rhythm*. Exactly what he intended remains a matter of some dispute, but fundamentally he was reviving metric strategies found in Greek and Latin podic verse and in Old English poetry (most famously in *Beowulf*). Instead of a line structure in which stressed syllables recur at regular intervals–what he called "running rhythm"– Hopkins advocated a line defined by a fixed number of stresses, but in which the feet contain varying numbers of unstressed syllables. Subsequent poets of the twentieth century, such as Robinson Jeffers and Marianne Moore, were to evolve similar prosodic approaches based on constant stresses and inconstant unstressed syllables. (Perhaps significantly, most, like Bryant, had studied ancient Greek poetry, in which the *paeon*, a four-syllable foot, consists of shifting combinations: one fully stressed, one lightly stressed, and two unstressed.) Hopkins apparently was not familiar with Bryant's poetry. And to postulate that Bryant influenced the Moderns would be quite far-fetched: indeed, misguided in their reading of him as a "Fireside Poet," twentieth-century American poets dismissed Bryant as a poetaster who fed the public pedestrian homilies. In 1915, Harriet Monroe, the editor of Chicago's influential *Poetry*, savagely attacked him in her magazine and in *The Dial*. That anyone in the rising generation Monroe championed might have looked upon him as a precursor is almost unimaginable. Yet the similarity in approach to meter is notable. Like Monroe's contemporaries, Bryant revisited tradition to discover principles for poetry's revitalization, and although no school of poets recognized the radical character of his prosody and formed around it, he was in fact far in advance of his time.

None of Bryant's poems displays his virtuosity more than "Thanatopsis"–especially the opening section, added when it was published in *Poems*. Meter implies a balanced pace, but here the poet calibrates imbalance; in its progress, the poem resembles a walk upon a file of seesaw planks of varied lengths. The first verse–"To him who in the love of Nature holds"–establishes a ten-syllable pattern, but this is immediately varied with eleven-syllable second and third verses, and even though the first foot is an iamb in a pentameter verse, most feet are not iambic, and the verses are consistently irregular. Millions of schoolchildren have read the line in the metronomic regularity they were taught, stressing *him, in, love, Na-,* and *holds*, yet sense insists that *who* be a one-syllable foot, followed by an anapest, and that *Nature* be the close of a parenthetical phrase. Expectation is next upset by *holds*: for an instant it seems a synonym for "believes"–the end stop to the address to the person who has faith in the love of Nature. Instead the verse is enjambed. It is not *love* which is held, but, as the object of a suddenly different meaning of the verb, *communion*. (Bryant will do the same thing in the next verse with *speaks*, which one takes as intransitive before it becomes transitive, with its object in the next line. Enjambment occurs in over half the poem, and a line's last word often undergoes a similar shift in syntax.)

The second verse–"Communion with her visible forms, she speaks"–both echoes and counters the first. The strictly separated four syllables *Com-mu-ni-on* correspond to the poem's initial four syllables; normal pronunciation, however, compresses the word into three syllables, thereby rhyming the elision, *-munion*, with the sharply detached syllables *who in* of the preceding line. Although the force of the rhyme is diminished by that detachment, it still serves to post the six-syllable set *with her visible forms* in parallel to *in the love of Nature*. The object of "she speaks"–"A various language"–completes the independent clause as the third six-syllable set, each consisting, in differing order, of a major stress, a minor stress, and four unstressed syllables.

Intricacy of composition extends throughout this opening passage. *doca iv?* The vowel of *To* and *who* repeats in the second syllable of *Communion*, and again in *beauty* and *musings* in the fifth and sixth lines. Lines four, five, and six end in near rhymes *smile*, *glides*, and *mild*. In addition, *mild*, in alliterating with *musings*, becomes a bridge between the keynote vowel and the linked sets of internal rhymes in lines seven and eight—*heal-* and *steals*; *Their*, *ere*, and *aware*, with *aware* echoing the previous line's *away*—that conclude the long reference to the unspecified "him" of the poem's opening prepositional phrase.

> and she glides
> Into his darker musings, with a mild
> And healing sympathy, that steals away
> Their sharpness, ere he is aware.

The taut complexity in this section distinguishes it from what follows. After the period, although the poem still proceeds in the poet's voice, the pronoun for the one addressed changes from third person to second, and apparently to mark the shift, no rhyme occurs throughout the sentence. Then, at the halfway point in line seventeen—precisely where the poem fragment as published in 1817 started—Nature speaks directly to *thee*, which, as if to signal another change (this time in the speaker), is rhymed with *see* within the next line. Here the rhyme serves to emphasize the finality of the two words that follow: *no more*. Over the course of the rest of the poem—sixty-five lines—Bryant employs no rhymes at all and relatively little assonance. This has the effect of casting Nature's pronouncement in as artlessly stark and unconsoling a guise as the truth of death it describes.

Despite their distinctive character, the idiosyncracies in "Thanatopsis" were not crafted for use as a standard template. Bryant ranged widely during his first, and most fruitful, decade as a poet. At times, he experimented within the shell of convention. In the thirty-seven couplets of "Rizpah," for instance, each line contains four accented feet, and most feet are iambs, yet no line is wholly in iambic tetrameter. The poem begins in dactyls, and the first foot of the second line is an anapest; as all lines contain either nine or ten syllables, trisyllabic feet abound in what Edgar Allan Poe, reviewing the poem years later in 1837, disparaged as a "fidgetty rhythm" yielding the "most positively disagreeable" effect.* Regardless of whether the effect pleases or not, however, "Rizpah" (like "Green River," probably written six years earlier and also in iambic tetrameter couplets) exhibits an emphatically rhythmic quality that is augmented by the variation. Elsewhere, Bryant strives for the opposite result–for example, in "Inscription for the Entrance to a Wood" (an early poem not yet titled when it was submitted with "Thanatopsis" to the *North American Review* in 1817) which, though metrically similar to "Thanatopsis," employs tonal deflections and alternations in cadence, combined with an often complex syntax, as dampers to the tempo, driving the lines toward prose. Yet, contrary to what this attraction toward relatively radical notions might suggest, Bryant showed no less zest for writing in a familiar vein. Such poems as "The Yellow Violet," "To a Waterfowl," "Oh Fairest of the Rural Maids," and "A Walk at Sunset," all published during the same period, hew to well-worn custom.

At a time when the few American critics who scrutinized poetry were still faulting Wordsworth for laxness and Byron for audacity, Bryant knew that unconventional prosody would rally no applause among his countrymen. The popularity and esteem he had been building since 1821 were gathered in spite of his "lapses" from the norm, not because of them. Even a fervid early booster, Willard Phillips, warned his close friend against indulging his "too great fondness for trisyllabics," lest he upset his readers' habits. But Bryant was insistent in his advocacy of liberating the poet's voice from simplistic constriction. "He who has got no further than *rúm ti* knows no more of versification than he who has merely learned the Greek alphabet knows Greek," he wrote, deriding his critics' pretensions, and he considered extending "On Trisyllabic Feet" into a dissertation that would instruct his audience in prosody's manifold complexities. Presumably, he meant more than a catalogue of their mechanics. Just as he eschewed "a diction much too florid and stately, and too far removed from the common idiom of our tongue," he strove to avoid "capricious departures from the natural construction" of that idiom in order to fit

---

*Poe's judgment on this version of the Old Testament story of a mother who stands guard over her slain sons is quite to the point: "The subject, we think, derives no additional interest from its poetical dress."

words to meter. Poetry, he believed, should spring from the music of speech, not be beaten into measures with a stick.

Attention to the rhythms of speech and relaxation of poetic conventions do not in themselves add up to free verse, of course, but they clearly lead in that direction. Although Bryant's assignment to the ranks of the Fireside Poets carelessly gainsays a common thread with the emancipatory "barbaric yawp" of *Leaves of Grass* in 1855, his link to Whitman, a quarter century his junior, is actually vibrant. Indeed, he was not only Whitman's favorite poet but also the one who most influenced him. When "Paumanok"–as he then styled himself–began writing poetry in 1840, he cleaved to sentiments expressed in "Thanatopsis" and the rest of Bryant's poems that proposed an impersonal unity with nature as the anodyne for death's intimidating reality.

Much has been made, with evident justification, of Emerson's role in bringing the "seething" Whitman to a "boil"–as the young poet acknowledged in his famous ingratiating letter. In 1842, Whitman had attended the lecture Emerson would soon publish as "The Poet," containing the famous maxim that "it is not metres, but a metre-making argument, that makes a poem." And Emerson's huzzah in responding to a presentation copy of the first edition of *Leaves of Grass* in 1855, "I greet you at the beginning of a great career," resoundingly suggests recognition of the eager acolyte by the master–just as Whitman intended when he reproduced the full congratulatory text in the second edition. Yet the obvious esteem in which he held Emerson should not obscure his more nutritive association with Bryant. It is most unlikely that Whitman had read Emerson's poems before their publication as a book in 1847, but even if he had, he would have found them, in form at least, quite unexceptional. Despite the ukases Emerson issued for an original American art and for poets who dared "threaten to abolish all that was called poetry," he promulgated no revolutionary models. That prospect had been more quietly advanced by Bryant. And although it is Emerson's fanfare that plays in the history books, it should be borne in mind that Whitman had also sent a copy of *Leaves of Grass* to Bryant, whose good opinion, had it been pronounced, might have mattered much more to him. Clearly, he had reason to expect it.

The two men had met in the 1840's, probably first at a Manhattan 1841 Democratic rally in which Whitman delivered a controversial speech that the *Evening Post* featured in its report. Seven months later, the newspaper praised a Whitman short story published in the *Democratic Review*. At some point shortly thereafter, their acquaintance developed a measure of intimacy. When Bryant died over three decades later, Whitman remembered warmly that the owner of the Manhattan paper several times crossed by ferry to Brooklyn and joined him on "rambles miles long." They had much in common. Whitman identified himself almost mystically with Long Island–as attested by "Paumanok," the Indian name for the island he had adopted as a *nom de plume*–and Bryant, in 1843, had bought forty acres in the village of Mosquito Cove at Hempstead Harbor, which he renamed Roslyn when he remodeled an old Quaker farmhouse into Cedarmere as the family home. Given their professional involvement in journalism–Whitman worked for several area newspapers and was editor of the *New York Aurora* in 1842 and of the *Brooklyn Eagle* from 1846 to 1848–the frothy newspaper scene provided them much gossip to exchange. Moreover, both were ardent Jacksonian Democrats who held similar political positions on the major issues of the day, and Bryant pointedly complimented Whitman in 1847 for having produced an *Eagle* that "breathed the true sentiments of the democracy." But their fellowship surely owed substantially to their literary activity. In 1850-51, the *Evening Post* would publish three Whitman essays and two or more of his poems, and although the selections were not necessarily decided by Bryant, they probably met with at least his tempered approval. On Whitman's side, his opinion of Bryant soared well beyond his customary flattery. When Bryant returned to New York after a journey through the American heartland, Whitman hailed him in an 1846 *Eagle* editorial, not just as the preeminent American poet, but as one who "stands among the first in the world." Indeed, Whitman continued, this exemplary American was so good that he considered moderating his praise just to make it credible. Those countrymen who stinted their commendation he dismissed as "literary quacks."

Tracing a young poet's indebtedness through adoption of a senior poet's meter tends to lead over rather supposititious ground, and Whitman's insistence on his originality may further weigh against the claim. ("The style of these poems," Whitman wrote anonymously about his own collection, " is simply their own style, just born and red. Nature may have given the hint to the author of 'Leaves of Grass,' but there exists no book or fragment of a book which can have given the hint to them.") But this is self-serving nonsense. Whitman's evolution demonstrates that he looked upon his idol as a mentor, even though he was not so quick to exploit the full possibilities in Bryant's departures from metric orthodoxy.

Whitman's early poems, besides reflecting a similar view of death as rest in a final return to nature, favor iambic tetrameter, also frequently used by Bryant. But it is other, less general aspects of Bryant that begin to surface in Whitman's poetry as it starts veering toward *Leaves of Grass*. Consider, for example, the initial stanza of Whitman's "New Year's Day, 1848":

> A morning fair: A noontide dubious:
> Then gathering clouds obscure the Sun:
> Then rain in torrents falls, subsiding soon
> Into a gentle dropping. By eve the sun
> Sinks into a cloudless west; and a mild breeze
> With pleasant motion stirs the atmosphere.
> Next in the blue vault above the moon and stars
> Vie in bright emulation to destroy the gloom of night.

The creation of a continuous present by registering a long series of immediate images evokes Bryant's "Summer Wind," published in the *United States Literary Gazette* twenty-four years earlier, and although the older poem is in blank verse, its lines, like Whitman's, seem ruled by the rhythms of ordinary speech:

> It is a sultry day; the sun has drunk
> The dew that lay upon the morning grass;
> There is no rustling in the lofty elm
> That canopies my dwelling, and its shade
> Scarce cools me. All is silent, save the faint
> And interrupted murmur of the bee,
> Settling on the sick flowers, and then again
> Instantly on the wing. The plants around
> Feel the too potent fervors: the tall maize
> Rolls up its long green leaves; the clover droops
> Its tender foliage, and declines its blooms.

Without much straining, one can also espy adumbrations of Whitman in the poet-self's sensual intrusion into the scene Bryant imbues with sexual anticipation:

                                                For me, I lie
Languidly in the shade, where the thick turf,
Yet virgin from the kisses of the sun,
Retains some freshness, and I woo the wind
That still delays his coming. Why so slow,
Gentle and voluble spirit of the air?
Oh, come and breathe upon the fainting earth
Coolness and life! Is it that in his caves
He hears me? See, on yonder woody ridge,
The pine is bending his proud top, and now
Among the nearer groves, chestnut and oak
Are tossing their green boughs about. He comes;
Lo, where the grassy meadow runs in waves!
The deep distressful silence of the scene
Breaks up with mingling of unnumbered sounds
And universal motion. He is come,
Shaking a shower of blossoms from the shrubs, ...

"The Prairies," perhaps Bryant's last great poem of his early period,
written in 1832after his return from a journey to Illinois to visit his
brothers, exercised an evidently more profound influence. From first to
last, the language is vatic, and the poet conveys a mystical experience
of union with his nation's land:

        These are the gardens of the Desert, these
The unshorn fields, boundless and beautiful,
For which the speech of England has no name–
The Prairies. I behold them for the first,
And my heart swells, while the dilated sight
Takes in the encircling vastness. Lo! they stretch,
In airy undulations, far away,
As if the ocean, in his gentlest swell,
Stood still, with all his rounded billows fixed,
And motionless forever.   .   .   .   .   .   .

                                                I listen long
To his domestic hum, and think I hear
The sound of that advancing multitude
Which soon shall fill these deserts. From the ground
Comes up the laugh of children, the soft voice
Of maidens, and the sweet and solemn hymn
Of Sabbath worshippers. The low of herds
Blends with the rustling of the heavy grain

> Over the dark brown furrows. All at once
> A fresher wind sweeps by, and breaks my dream,
> And I am in the wilderness alone.

Here, too, are the linked rolls famously associated with Whitman but which do not make a conspicuous entrance until he embarks on *Leaves of Grass*. Bryant's citation, within a dozen lines, of clouds that sweep with their shadows, causing the land's surface to undulate and the hollows to seem to glide and chase sunny ridges, and of Southern breezes that toss golden and flame-like flowers and pass a prairie-hawk that flaps his wings "yet moves not"–breezes that have played among Mexican palms and Texan vines and have "crisped" brooks gliding from Sonora origins to the Pacific–could make easy accommodation in Whitman's assertion of physical America as itself a poem transmitted through his words. The thesis that Whitman's anaphoric catalogues derive from Bryant, and particularly from this poem so radically similar in intent to Whitman's emerging vision of his poetic relationship to his vast, vital native country, is both patent and far more compelling than has ever been recognized.

Bryant's effect on Whitman extended well beyond poetic devices. At the end of March 1851, when Whitman was most actively transforming his poetry, he addressed the Brooklyn Art Union on the importance of art and the artist.[*] Although retrospective commentary on the speech has traced it to roots in Emerson, the one poem he quoted was not Emerson's "Ode to Beauty," or "Painting and Sculpture," or "The Problem" but Bryant's "A Forest Hymn." Given the topic of the address, it seems a strange context to invoke:

> Lo! all grow old and die–but see again,
> How on the faltering footsteps of decay
> Youth presses–ever gay and beautiful youth
> In all its beautiful forms. These lofty trees
> Wave not less proudly that their ancestors
> Moulder beneath them. Oh, there is not lost
> One of earth's charms: upon her bosom yet,

---

[*]Not only the invitation to speak but also the nomination to head the Brooklyn Art Union to which it led may have been attributable to Bryant, himself a patron of the arts and the man who introduced Whitman to Charles L. Heyde, the accomplished painter who later married Hannah Louisa, Whitman's favorite sister.

After the flight of untold centuries,
The freshness of her far beginning lies
And yet shall lie.

Jerome Loving, an excellent recent Whitman biographer, gives a pass to this apparent incongruity but calls attention to another: the speech's ending, in which Whitman quotes from his own poem, "Resurgemus," a tribute to the fallen in Europe's failed revolutions of 1848 that has no relationship to the role of art. Why, Loving asks, this "remarkable" leap? How does assurance that freedom's seed is growing and will in turn bear seed convert into a metaphor for art's persistence and indomitability? Loving supposes the answer lies in "The Poet," where, about midway through the essay, Emerson refers to "Genius [as] the activity which repairs the decay of things," and to Nature's insuring the survival of even its most humble manifestations, such as the agaric mushroom. But Loving's presumed analogy between genius and nature on the one hand and the dream of liberty and the impulse of art on the other seems highly friable. A more intriguing explanation, more plausible though also conjectural, rests on Whitman's ties to Bryant. His recitation from "A Forest Hymn" in the Brooklyn address points to another of Bryant's primeval forest settings–the one that frames "The Antiquity of Freedom." Written in 1842, this Bryant poem arose from the same political turmoil that would produce the armed struggle for liberty saluted in "Resurgemus," the other poem Whitman quoted for his audience. More than a common fervent interest in Europe's great political upheavals may account for the conjunction.

"Resurgemus" marks Whitman's transition from his novitiate years to his bold emergence as a fully formed poet. First published in 1850, this pivotal work would be reissued in altered form five years later in *Leaves of Grass*–the only poem in that 1855 edition to have appeared previously. Curiously, "The Antiquity of Freedom" had been produced during a similar transition for Bryant–though mainly unrealized and of lesser magnitude. For about a decade, the man acknowledged as America's foremost poet had also been faulted for his limited scope and for a failure of ambition. He "lacked passion." He was satisfied with "prettied" subjects. He was preoccupied with describing nature. In 1832, the *Foreign Quarterly Review*, while not contesting his place at the head of American poets, found him "not a writer of marked originality," and it decided it could do no better than to "assign him an honourable station in the second class." Edgar Allan Poe, reviewing *Poems* in 1837, noted this continuing critical "equivocation" and echoed it: he was a poet for "the mere enjoyment of the beautiful"—and little more. What praise he granted, he also discounted: "In all the *minor* merits, Mr. Bryant is pre-eminent" (italics added). Nine years later, Poe, trying to make amends, still could not muster more than restrained praise in refuting Bryant's disparagers: "It will never do to claim for Bryant a genius of the loftiest order, but there has been latterly, since the days of Mr. Longfellow and Mr. Lowell, a growing disposition to deny him *genius* in *any* respect." In part, enthusiasm for Bryant's poetry had ebbed because wearying duties at the *Evening Post* kept him from nurturing his poetic career, but it was also evident that the public had become all too familiar with his verse. As Poe astutely observed, he was being "overlooked by modern schools, because deficient in those externals which have become in a measure symbolical of those schools."

Bryant was well aware that he was fading from favor, and his friend Dana, like a growing number of his impatient critics, candidly advised him that the time had come to burnish his reputation by tackling a major work. Bryant was never one to discuss his poetic intentions with non-poets, but the evidence indicates that he had come to the same conclusion. Parke Godwin, his son-in-law and biographer, believed he had embarked on a plan for a long, elaborate work presenting "the aspects of American nature and life as they are seen from the shores of Massachusetts to the prairies of the great West," connected by personal narrative. Although Godwin admitted that the dimensions of this project were conjectural, Bryant certainly did execute some substantial portion of it, which he published, in part, in *The Fountain and Other Poems* in 1842, stating in his introduction that the remainder "may possibly be finished hereafter."

Bryant specifically identified only two poems as salvaged from the uncompleted design, the title poem and "An Evening Revery," but he alluded to others as well, all in the blank verse he stated would be the grand mosaic's consistent meter. "The Antiquity of Freedom" and "The Painted Cup," both composed at this time, were probably part of the plan, and it is likely that "The Old Man's Counsel," written two years earlier, was to have provided an autobiographical reference for the poet personally present in the other poems. In addition, two works written in 1842 but published in *The White Footed Deer* in 1844–"Noon," a fragment, and "Hymn of the Sea"–almost certainly were conceived as sections of the grand tapestry. The few Bryant scholars and even fewer modern critics who have paid any heed to these poems have given them short shrift, and it would indeed be difficult to argue that they exhibit a rejuvenated gift. Missing are the energy and the tautness that once distinguished his best verse. Even Dana, apparently acquainted with Bryant's intention to produce an extended work consisting of inter-related parts, confessed disappointment in *The Fountain*: "Have you a poem with some few passages of more stir and passion (I don't mean of convulsions) than these? If your poem is long, it will need have here and there a peak thrown up out of the level."

Yet Bryant's concept clearly aimed at a grand scope that his writing had lacked since "The Ages," and although he failed to sustain his inspiration through to realization of his ambitious theme, it would reemerge after a decade through another poet. What Bryant had germinated would grow as *Leaves of Grass*. Whitman biographers have occasionally questioned his professions of close friendship with Bryant, and impeached as an old man's garrulous embroidery his fond recollections of losing themselves in discussions on their long walks. In fact, there are no grounds for impugning his truthfulness in these accounts–and ample corroborating evidence. One can even detect in Whitman's memories of Bryant's strolls from one New York City men's club to another, gathering affection as American's "good gray poet," proleptically the very image Whitman would craft for himself. Is it likely that the lion who was seeking to revive his literary significance through a cycle of poems driven by a new vision would discourse about his ideas with an eager, aspiring poet who venerated him? Despite his normal reticence, it seems the failure to do so would be more unlikely.

Whitman's explicit and implicit invocation in his Brooklyn Art Union lecture of Bryant's religious regard for nature and his apostolic faith in democracy as an evolving force in history–twin themes Bryant had been striving to bring together in his uncompleted major poem–points directly toward *Leaves of Grass*. More persuasive of a vital link between the two men at this transitional juncture in their careers, however, are some of the poems Bryant had expected would meld in an American panorama viewed through a lens of the self. It is almost impossible to read "An Evening Revery," among others, and not hear intimations of Whitman's chant.

In bright alcoves,
In woodland cottages with barky walls,
In noisome cells of the tumultuous town,
Mothers have clasped with joy the new-born babe.
Graves by the lonely forest, by the shore
Of rivers and of ocean, by the ways
Of the thronged city, have been hollowed out
And filled, and closed. This day hath parted friends
That ne'er before were parted; it hath knit
New friendships; it hath seen the maiden plight
Her faith, and trust her peace to him who long
Had wooed; and it hath heard, from lips which late
Were eloquent of love, the first harsh word,
That told the wedded one her peace was flown.

Similarly, "Noon," extending the celebration of Earth's boundless being found in "The Prairie," becomes more characteristic of Whitman's crescendos of observation than of what had once been the typical product of Bryant's pen:

I, too, amid the overflow of day,
Behold the power which wields and cherishes
The frame of Nature. From this brow of rock
That overlooks the Hudson's western marge,
I gaze upon the long array of groves,
The piles and gulfs of verdure drinking in
The grateful heats. They love the fiery sun;
Their broadening leaves grow glossier, and their sprays
Climb as he looks upon them. In the midst,
The swelling river, into his green gulfs,
Unshadowed save by passing sails above,
Takes the redundant glory, and enjoys
The summer in his chilly bed. Coy flowers,
That would not open in the early light,
Push back their plaited sheaths. The rivulet's pool,
That darkly quivered all the morning long
In the cool shade, now glimmers in the sun;
And o'er its surface shoots, and shoots again,
The glittering dragon-fly, and deep within
Run the brown water-beetles to and fro. –

A silence, the brief sabbath of an hour,
Reigns o'er the fields; the laborer sits within

His dwelling; he has left his steers awhile,
Unyoked, to bite the herbage, and his dog
Sleeps stretched beside the door-stone in the shade.
Now the gray marmot, with uplifted paws,
No more sits listening by his den, but steals
Abroad, in safety, to the clover-field,
And crops its juicy blossoms. All the while
A ceaseless murmur from the populous town
Swells o'er these solitudes: a mingled sound
Of jarring wheels, and iron hoofs that clash
Upon the stony ways, and hammer-clang,
And creak of engines lifting ponderous bulks,
And calls and cries, and tread of eager feet,
Innumerable, hurrying to and fro.

As if to announce a transformation from his early poetry to the aesthetics he now embraced, Bryant wrote "The Painted Cup," published in *The Fountain*, though evidently either meant for inclusion in his long poem or composed as a playful diversion from it. Beginning in a manner Whitman would make his own, the poet's eye ranges over the landscape, and then rests on the eponymous flower:

The fresh savannas of the Sangamon
Here rise in gentle swells, and the long grass
Is mixed with rustling hazels. Scarlet tufts
Are glowing in the green, like flakes of fire;
The wanderers of the prairie know them well,
And call that brilliant flower the Painted Cup.

Here Bryant pauses and changes his address. What, he asks, is art to do with this selected object? One possibility would be to surrender it to the sort of imagination traditionally associated with poets—a mode to which he himself had not been entirely immune. But this would only result in clichés, and so he rejects it.

Now, if thou art a poet, tell me not
That these bright chalices were tinted thus
To hold the dew for fairies, when they meet
On moonlight evenings in the hazel-bowers,
And dance till they are thirsty. Call not up,
Amid this fresh and virgin solitude,
The faded fancies of an elder world;

Instead, he invokes a wondrous reality, the immediate beauty of multifarious nature.

> But leave these scarlet cups to spotted moths
> Of June, and glistening flies, and humming-birds,
> To drink from, when on all these boundless lawns
> The morning sun looks hot. Or let the wind
> O'erturn in sport their ruddy brims, and pour
> A sudden shower upon the strawberry-plant,
> To swell the reddening fruit that even now
> Breathes a slight fragrance from the sunny slope.

And yet, finally, he recognizes that the poet in himself craves something more than the materialistic pleasure of sensations.

> But thou art of a gayer fancy. Well—
> Let then the gentle Manitou of flowers,
> Lingering amid the bloomy waste he loves,
> Though all his swarthy worshippers are gone—
> Slender and small, his rounded cheek all brown
> And ruddy with the sunshine; let him come
> On summer mornings, when the blossoms wake,
> And part with little hands the spiky grass,
> And touching, with his cherry lips, the edge
> Of these bright beakers, drain the gathered dew.

At the simplest level of understanding, this last stanza concedes, back-handedly, the ascendency of the poet's "gayer fancy" over mere observation of the real world, but it also intimates something more than a whimsical acknowledgment of the power of whimsy. Why did Bryant abandon his ambitious project? He left no explanation, but it seems clear that he had difficulty resolving poems that consisted of open-ended recitation of what the panoptic "I" beholds. "The Painted Cup" avoids this problem by being, at bottom, about the problem and not about the flower. But that clever turn quickly hit its limits.

What drew Bryant intellectually to compose verse was some particular manifestation illustrating the working of Nature's "Manitou." That he had come to his literary appreciation of nature through an early mastery of homeopathic medicine may not be entirely coincidental. (He had been named after William Cullen, whose writing led to the elaboration of homeopathy, based on the Law of Similars; his father, himself a homeopath, trained his son in gathering simples.

Bryant remained an adept, and decades later served as president of the Homeopathic Society of New York Physicians.) The notion that an herb could hold the power to cure by triggering restoration of the harmony underlying nature's goodness is not far removed from the concept of a poem as a moral lesson to be derived from observation of some part of nature. Thus: the yellow violet teaches the virtue of loyalty to those who shared humble beginnings; the fringed gentian, hope in the face of bleak fatality; the anemone, the value of seeking instruction in out of the way places; etc. And in a broader manner, nature supplies the metaphors that illustrate vital truths: a rivulet represents both life's passage and its renewal; wild, stormy March is "a welcome month" because it reminds us that regeneration follows a bleak prospect; the West Wind is an emblem of careless joy, unfettered youth, and credulous love; the hurricane intimates the terror of uncertainty furiously loosed from beyond the familiar confines of experience. In all these poems, the role of the poet is to compose the images by which sensory experience guides toward wisdom.

Not all of Bryant's poetry falls under this classification, of course. Some of his best early poems–"Inscription for the Entrance to a Wood," "A Forest Hymn," and, indeed, "Thanatopsis"–develop simple abstract ideas toward a broadly philosophical purpose. In that respect, they are not dissimilar to a larger portion of his later poems, which are generally much weaker. Part of the explanation for the decline is a tendency to rest content with shopworn language that dulls the emergent idea. For example, in "The Unknown Way," written in 1845, the poet walks where sands "glow," the path is "dusty," the branches "play," the brook is "silvery," the vale is "shady" and the shade is "cool," the hall is "stately," the track is "weary." And he sees lovers "stray" on "lonely walks" "Till the tender stars appear." With no foreshadowing, all this to take the poet to where he hears "the voice of the mighty Sea," and asks, "Dost thou, oh path of the woodland! / End where those waters roar, / Like human life, on a trackless beach, / With a boundless Sea before?" Even so, the greater general fault in the later poems is the loss of the remarkable sensitivity to the properties of speech, exploited through complex patterns and manipulation of sound, which once made his verse fresh and intriguing.

Although the line between Bryant and Whitman–not only in their devotion as poets to the irrepressible extension of democracy, their embrace of America's destiny, their hymn-like celebration of life, and their transcendentalist view of the physical world but also in their attraction to the sense of meter as the song of speech–has remained almost completely hidden from critical consciousness, Bryant's legacy to another main branch of our poetic tradition has been neglected because it is so obvious. Robert Frost was raised on Bryant (as well as on Wordsworth, Emerson, and Longfellow), and he had heard his mother recite "To a Waterfowl" to him so many times that, at twelve, he realized he knew it by heart, despite never having tried to commit it to memory. Biographers have also recorded Frost's taking the affirmative in a high school debate on the question: "Resolved: William Cullen Bryant is a better poet than John Greenleaf Whittier." It is easy to make too much of this occurrence, but one should not dismiss it too lightly, either. From an early age, Frost was committed to poetry, and although his tastes were immature, he consciously studied what made a poem work. Bryant offered a veritable primer. And once Frost chose to be a poet, he also studied the appropriate role he would act. There, too, Bryant presented an example.

Just as Whitman found in Bryant his model of the Good Gray Poet he wished to become, Frost, relatively sophisticated and raised in city ways, saw in the urbane New York City editor whose poems focused on country matters an appealing rustic persona he, too, could construct. Through no deliberate design, Bryant was not just a poet who had been born and raised in New England; he was a New England poet. Frost, deliberately, cut his cloth to the same measure. Of course, there was more to the resemblance than adapting to a type. The contents page of a Frost collection could easily be mistaken for a list of Bryant's titles, and a poem like "Two Graves" obviously foreshadows Frost. Coincidence, too, has conspired to lay the two poets' statements of America's appointed destiny, "The Ages" and "The Gift Outright," symmetrically at defining public events at opposite ends of their careers. More pertinently, their poems tend to show a similar structure. Frost learned more than the words of "To a Waterfowl": he also absorbed a sense of "the figure a poem makes." His famous statement that a poem "begins in delight and ends in wisdom" perfectly fits Bryant's transition from the question posed by an arresting image in that poem's opening quatrain to the often-quoted assurance based on the "lesson" at the close. To be sure, the concept of a poem as a moral or philosophical inference drawn from an isolated natural object (conventionally a flower or a bird) did not originate with Bryant: poetry, after all, is rooted in metaphor–the statement of one thing in terms of another–and Romantic sensibilities that began waxing in the eighteenth century dictated not only a huge shift toward nature as a poetic subject but also a transformation in the perception of nature as a spiritual manifestation and as a source of the harmony lost through social upheaval. That said, however, it is also clear that Bryant, even more than those poets immediately in his train, represented the tradition that schooled Frost and other American poets over the course of about a century.

Bryant gave American poetry two powerful impulses. One relates to subject matter. Both nature and rural ways have attracted a nimbus of sanctity in our national imagination. Hamilton's financial genius and his *Report on Manufactures* laid the foundations for the emerging nation's economic strength, but we prefer to construe our identity in terms of the Jeffersonian yeoman farmer. Our literature has shown the same proclivity. At precisely the time New England was exploiting every flow of its abundant streams and rivers to drive its mills and generate wealth, the transcendentalists were concentrating on the divinity behind the world's natural surface. Of all the writers of the American Renaissance, only Melville, and only in one story, takes his readers inside a factory. In the post-Civil War period, when industrialization was exploding at an accelerating pace, our preeminent writer was concluding–through Huck, his fantasy self–that society was too compromised morally to be borne, and he might yet "light out for the territory." *A Connecticut Yankee in King Arthur's Court* renders the same judgment: "progress" serves only to expose man's ancient evil. And Mark Twain is not an anomaly. No major writer during a span of almost half a century depicted the pressing reality of the new urban, industrial America. Our imaginative instinct has always tended to favor refuge in Arcadia.

In "Green River," as a young lawyer beset by the nettlesome duties of a profession he was discovering he loathed, Bryant declared that "steal[ing] an hour" to join the river "in silent dream" afforded relief from being "forced to drudge for the dregs of men" and mingling with "the sons of strife." That spiritual yearning for sanctuary in nature persisted during the years he not only owned and directed the most prestigious newspaper in the nation but also involved himself in the affairs of all levels of government. Reviewing *The Fountain* in 1842, Harvard professor Charles Felton noted the contrast between the "torrents of invective" that Bryant the engaged political activist poured out and "the smiling fields" that the poet produced without a hint "of the furious din with which he was just surrounded." He viewed poetry as a "field" in which to appreciate beauty and discern examples of good sense, not as a ground for disputation. And Americans have generally agreed. Like Frost in the next century, Bryant had a dark side in his reflections, but the public refused to see it, embracing and loving him instead for the comfort they wanted him to provide.

No one writer, or artist, or philosopher should be credited for the eruption of American interest in nature, but Bryant was among those who affected the way his countrymen regarded the world beyond the settlements' edge. Asher Durand's iconic painting, "Kindred Spirits," shows Thomas Cole pointing with his walking stick toward the Kaaterskill Falls and the equally famous Kaaterskill Clove, presumably discoursing while Bryant listens. But this depiction slightly misleads. After meeting in New York City in 1821, the two men formed a friendship that mutually nourished their arts for the rest of Cole's short life. Although it was Cole who founded the Hudson River School, generally acknowledged as having fostered a fascination with wilderness that extended into a Romantic veneration of our West, Bryant's inspiration provided a collateral force. When his friend died in 1848, Bryant delivered a long funeral oration that reiterated a lifetime of praise for Cole as the first American artist to capture the nation's "wild magnificence" and convey its implicit moral teaching. Of course, Bryant strove for the same qualities in much of his own work—a poem such as "A Scene on the Banks of the Hudson" can be read as a verse version of a Cole canvas. The sensibilities developed by Bryant and the artists with whom he made common cause reflect something fundamentally American. If the national parks created at the start of the twentieth century preserve a portion of the pristine beauty of our continent before its conquest by Europeans, they also serve as natural cathedrals of that faith of prelapsarian goodness Bryant evangelized to counter the Calvinist gospel of nature as the lure of the Devil. "Hymn" in his titles of poems is intended not as analogue but literally as religious utterance.

Bryant's second major contribution lay in transforming our understanding of prosody. He was the first American poet to seek the music in the patterns of ordinary speech and to adapt the measure to those patterns instead of fitting the words mechanically to the measure. And he was the first to appreciate the relationship of intonation to meter. Even before his close friendship in New York with Lorenzo DaPonte, Mozart's brilliant librettist, and the passion for Italian opera fostered by it, Bryant recognized the importance of phrasing. When one reads "Thanatopsis" or "Summer Wind" aloud and then compares the arrangement of its words with that of any poem by Poe or an American poet before 1821, the radical difference is immediately apparent. More than freeing the line from an obligatory regularity, or even permitting extra syllables in order to obey the commands of natural language, he conceived of the poet as a composer, as conscious of the importance of the spaces between his notes as of the length of those notes and the stress with which they should be sounded. What other poet of his time would not only have understood that "red west" and "green blade" in the fourth line of "An Evening Revery" must be said in different ways but also have known how to guide the voice toward those differences? Which of his contemporaries engineered so expertly the variations in metric feet as valves in the flow of thought?

To a twenty-first-century audience, Bryant's occasional "o'er" and "doth" and "ne'er" strikes an antique note, but it is the comparative rarity of those notes—as well as their diminishing frequency—that is noteworthy. No American poet of his time was more intent on retrieving poetry from artificiality. Similarly, he counseled the next generation "to go directly to nature for their imagery, instead of taking it from what had once been regarded as the common stock of the guild of poets." And he cautioned as well against being seduced by the abstractions of "stiff Latinisms." Words should be immediately evocative of the specific sensory quality of experience. Ironically, the very protagonists of twentieth-century Modernism who consigned Bryant to the past's dustier shelves would proclaim the same concept as basic to their revolutionary creed.

"The Eternal Flow of Things"

The study of Bryant's poetry might properly begin with a very early poem never published during his lifetime: "They Taught Me, and It Was a Fearful Creed." Its first line, which serves as its title, is most eloquent. "They," unidentified, immediately introduces an oppressive presence. The boy–clearly Bryant himself in tender years–has had imposed upon his "heart" a creed that induces only fear (the word occurs three times in five lines), "terrible doubt," and "horrible visions." The God of this creed is a parent who not only abandons his "creatures" but also "forgets" them, allowing the grave to smother and obliterate all that they have been or thought.

Bryant overcame the frail health of his childhood to play a consequential role in the affairs of his city and nation, yet almost nothing of that experience enters his poetry. Instead, his verse is driven by a sustained reaction to the fright of "eternal death" that had gripped his budding imagination. Guided by his sometimes-absent father, a physician with a "mild and indulgent temper" whose benevolent faith was under the sway of early transcendentalist and Unitarian thinkers in Boston, young Cullen found release from dour Calvinism doctrine in a religious concept of nature as the benign manifestation of an impersonal cosmic force. Throughout his life, his poems would affirm that faith, emphasizing the ebb and flow of all existence.

The writing of "Thanatopsis" may not have been coincident with his rejecting theism, but its success in launching his career established it as the poet's evangel of religious liberation. The poem's teaching accorded with ideas that had been rapidly gaining favor in the intellectual circles of eastern Massachusetts since the last decade of the previous century, but it is nonetheless remarkable that its vision did not offend orthodox Christians and bring a rain of condemnation from pulpits in less liberal sectors of the nation. Perhaps Bryant was spared because relatively few readers paid much attention to poetry. And perhaps, as is often the case in all times and places, many of those who did failed to comprehend what was being said, for "Thanatopsis" gainsays the afterlife that is the foundation of traditional religion. No heaven, no hell, no Day of Judgment—and thus, by extension, no salvation, or Jesus Christ, or even God the Father. It asserts only the material world of nature, and then deals with the implications.

Bryant at the start takes note of nature's pleasant aspect, "gladness" and the "smile and eloquence of beauty," but that same nature also presents him with the ineluctability of death, and its recognition blights the spirit. The rest of the poem explains "Nature's teachings" as an antidote to fear. Contrary to what has sometimes been written about "Thanatopsis," Nature's solace is not in its bounty or aesthetic delight but in what would conventionally be seen as terrifying: utter obliteration of the self, a negation of all egoism. "Each human trace" of "individual being" will be reclaimed as mere matter, "brother to the insensible rock" and mould to sustain vegetation. The same destiny awaits all who ever lived or ever will live, rendering all ambition—chasing a "favorite phantom"—as vanity. But this is not a message of despair. On the contrary. Unlike Thomas Gray's lament for unfulfilled lives in "Elegy Written in a Country Churchyard," to which "Thanatopsis" is often compared and wrongfully found similar, Bryant's poem celebrates the nothingness of death. Precisely because it is nothing, death makes it imperative to live, to exploit and enjoy life's possibilities unafraid, accountable only to our own consciences. The grave—an ending, not a portal to horror—thus becomes no worse than a couch on which to dream at day's close.

Bryant may have escaped denunciation of "Thanatopsis" because "To a Waterfowl," which accompanied it to the public's notice, offered such emphatic (and oft-quoted) declaration of what seems, in its concluding stanza, unmistakably to be faith in a theistic God:

> He who, from zone to zone,
> Guides through the boundless sky thy certain flight,
> In the long way that I must tread alone,
> Will lead my steps aright.

Other Bryant poems, early and late, also speak of God in ways that appear to refute the position stated in "Thanatopsis." In "Hymn to Death," a protest against the injustice of death meted out indiscriminately, he concludes, addressing his deceased father, "Rest, in the bosom of God, till the brief sleep / Of death is over, and a happier life / Shall dawn to waken thine insensible dust." Another obituary tribute, "Consumption," composed as his favorite sister lay dying, closed with "And we will trust in God to see thee yet again." Similarly, in "The Life That Is" (1858), after his wife had recovered from a near-fatal illness (and after his formal baptism), he expressed thanks that she had not yet been called to heaven, "Where He, who went before thee to prepare / For His meek followers, shall assign thy place." Three decades before, in "The Fringed Gentian," he had wished that, when the hour of his death approached, "Hope, blossoming within my heart, / May look to heaven as I depart." Such allusions are not rare. In addition, Bryant wrote a fair number of hymns in which, as one would expect, specifically Christian references occur. Was he, then, a Christian after all?

The question has no certain answer. That he practiced his version of occasional conformity seems obvious, for he attended services in Congregational, Presbyterian, and even Roman Catholic churches while subscribing as a Unitarian, the faith his father came to embrace. All the same, he refused to discuss his religious beliefs, despite frequent queries: "public display" of what was profoundly private, he insisted, was inappropriate. Reason ruled his mind, yet, as he conceded in "The Conjunction of Jupiter and Venus," he would not accept it as his tyrant, for "there are motions, in the mind of man, that [reason] must look upon with awe." Christ and belief in an afterlife clearly served psychological needs, and Bryant was not one to war against them. Scrutiny of the themes woven through his lifetime of poems, however, shows convictions far closer to pantheism than to any Christian sect. Even "To a Waterfowl," frequently cited to illustrate faith in God's loving direction of each separate life, should probably be read instead as an avowal of trust in the instincts the "Power" within nature provides. Written while Bryant was beset by doubt as to his life's course, the poem was more likely a means to muster the courage to act on his impulses (and, in the words of "Thanatopsis," to "chase his favorite phantom") than a statement of insouciant resignation to God's design.

At bottom, Bryant is a philosophical poet. As a Romantic, he has roots in both Plato and Aristotle, but the more distinct echo is Pre-Socratic; well before Emerson, as the closing couplet of "Mutation" (1824) attests, Bryant stood as the Heraclitus of American letters:

> Weep not that the world changes—did it keep
> A stable, changeless state, 'twere cause indeed to weep.

Death in his poems usually leads to the view of the universe as a "vast cycle of being." Intellectually, Bryant accepts death as the condition of life's continuance, even as his emotions resist that fatality. This essential tension finds its most vivid figure in his well-turned (yet little-known) "Earth's Children Cleave to Earth." There, a "wreath of mist," like human will, clings "from hold to hold" in its inexorable upward progress along the mutable world. The sun's rays lift it until, finally, it surrenders its identity to "the glorious sky." Thus the life-giving power in nature reclaims every sublunary creature into its timeless perfection, then to be reissued into the changing universe.

The mountain rivulet from which the mist rises in "Earth's Children" often recurs in Bryant's poetry, not only as a literal reference to the small brook that ran through the grounds of his Cummington home but also, implicitly, as imagery representing the span of a life. The metaphor has an unmistakable Heraclitean resonance. Famously misquoted by Plato as having said that no man steps into the same stream twice, Heraclitus actually wrote that what makes the stream constant is the inconstant water in its flow. Bryant's autobiographical "The Rivulet" builds on the same conceit. "Thou changest not–but I am changed," he says to the "little rill" he visits throughout his life. The children drawn to play on its banks, like its flowers and herbs, grow old, die, and are replaced in kind by others; the flow of life enjoys an "endless infancy" through replenishment of its particulars even as it carries the poet toward death. After almost two decades, he would invoke the same trope in "An Evening Revery":

> Gently, and without grief, the old shall glide
> Into the new; the eternal flow of things,
> Like a bright river of the fields of heaven,
> Shall journey onward in perpetual peace.

Sometimes, when the image is not of a stream (or of a river as in "The Night-Journey of a River"), the "flow" takes another form–such as "the struggling tides of life" in "The Crowded Street." Among his most poignant poems, "The Snow-Shower" pictures human lives as snowflakes in descent toward a dark lake–not just death but the collective deaths of all who ever lived; when all "rest in the dark and silent lake," however, a sunbeam falls upon it. As in "Thanatopsis," peace lies not in a delusive hope but in communion with the "great Movement of the Universe," and asserting it in poetry becomes a sacramental affirmation.

Bryant's Short Fiction: A Road Abandoned

If critical attention to William Cullen Bryant's poetry has been rare, notice of his short fiction, even as passing mentions, has been so scant as to approach invisibility. In part, this neglect reflects a dearth of scholarly interest in the traditional tale's evolution into the modern short story. But the more patent explanation is that Bryant chose to define himself as a poet. Story writing for him was a side activity, something prompted by his need to pad out a magazine or miscellany he edited, or the product of a literary divertissement he played with writers who were close friends. He never analyzed the dynamics of the short story as he had, with such assiduousness, the elements of poetry, and in the main his forays into short fiction betray that casual interest. Among his dozen titles, one finds extended anecdotes, imaginary reportage, ghost stories that turn into jokes, evocations of legend, and, in one instance, a simple character sketch, but very few which indicate an aesthetic purposiveness or firm grasp of form. "A Pennsylvania Legend" and "The Indian Spring" are two notable exceptions.

Oral stories, or traditional tales, have been transmitted throughout history, in cultures all over the world, and grand treasuries of them were written down and collected long before the invention of printing. The modern short story, however, drew sustenance from the institution of the magazine (essentially an American development, to which Americans applied their adaptation of an old word, meaning "storehouse"). Younger by about a century than the modern novel, the short story, like its grander relative, is primarily a literary artifact; its quality resides less in the events it describes—what is told—than in its creation of characters and in the manner of its telling. Many writers foreshadowed its appearance, but its acknowledged father is Washington Irving (who, paradoxically, did not write for magazines); his *Sketch Book* (1819-20), had a massive impact on literary history. It not only announced the arrival of a new form of writing but also inspired imitation in several

European countries as well as in its author's native land. Bryant's flirtations with short fiction owe directly to Irving's example.

Fair assessment of Bryant's stories needs to take account of their early dates of composition. The first of Nathaniel Hawthorne's tales to be published, "The Hollow of the Three Hills" and "An Old Woman's Tale" (printed in 1830, though probably written a short time earlier) are quite rudimentary. Shortly thereafter, Edgar Allan Poe began his career as a writer of tales with the undistinguished "MS Found in a Bottle" in 1833. Among those who emulated Irving in the decade following the success of *The Sketch Book*, James Kirke Paulding, his good friend, former collaborator, and chief rival, published *Tales of the Good Woman* in 1829. Long forgotten, Paulding's sketches and narratives drawing on New York's Dutch past strike no independent note; even the best of them are less inventive and ambitious than most of Bryant's varied attempts at short fiction. But one need not reach into the ranks of minor writers for comparisons that show Bryant to advantage: contrary to expectations, his small output stands up rather well even against Irving's own tales. "Rip Van Winkle" and "The Legend of Sleepy Hollow" are justly celebrated, but among the more than thirty other pieces in *The Sketch Book* that qualify as fiction, many display unbearably maudlin themes (e.g., "The Wife," "The Widow and Her Son") or build on trick plots (e.g., "The Spectre Bridegroom"). None of Bryant's stories is inferior to the major portion of *The Sketch Book*, and his best arguably match the best of Irving's subsequent volumes published in the 1820's, *Bracebridge Hall* and *Tales of a Traveller*.

"A Pennsylvania Legend," Bryant's initial attempt at fiction, composed in haste in 1825, sought to exploit the fashion Irving had recently set in his adaptation of the previous century's Gothic tale revival in Germany. Yet, although Bryant surely had Irving's Dutch colonists in mind in choosing German settlers in Pennsylvania as his characters, it is not quite an imitation. Bryant neither stipples his descriptions with Romantic local color nor executes the gentle turns of wit found in Irving's Knickerbocker pieces. These narratives also differ in their use of the supernatural. Plying the "sportive gothic," Irving seems to wink at his audience before either supplying or suggesting a rational, alternative explanation. Even in relating the uncanny, he makes style his foremost consideration, cultivating the pose of the detached gentleman in the manner of Addison and Steele. By comparison, Bryant's adaptation of the folk tale appears traditional—indeed, he devotes his opening paragraphs to a lament for the extinct superstitious belief that once excited and delighted the imagination. He is also more conventional in that, just as his poems tend to unfold lessons from observation, "A Pennsylvania Legend" is essentially a moral tale—an illustration of values. But Bryant's excursion into short fiction does not merely reach back to models from the past. In manipulating the reader's sympathies in regard to the protagonist and, whether by clever design or happenstance, advancing the story through the development of its symbols, he shows unusually modern aspects.

The tale's primary symbol is a deformity passed through generations of Buckels (*Buckel* is German for "hump"; *ein Buclige*, for "hunchback"). Customarily in folk tales, physical repulsiveness invites either of two opposing interpretations. The most common—the unsightly witch is an obvious instance—sees a misshapen body as corresponding to an iniquitous soul. The other—exemplified by ugly ducklings and hideous beasts of various sorts who turn into handsome princes—simultaneously appeals to a sensibility that believes it is misunderstood and out of sorts with the world while also warning against judgments based solely on appearances. Bryant's symbol initially operates in the first mode. Walter Buckel asserts descent from a milkmaid impregnated by a hump-backed baron. In his eyes, the hump warrants aristocratic arrogance, and when his neighbors in Germany express ridicule instead of honor, he emigrates to Pennsylvania. (*Den Buckel unterrutschen* translates as "Kiss my rump.") The Americans, true to their reputation as good, democratic neighbors, pay the Buckels' disfigurement no heed and welcome the family by building a humble log house for them. Walter, however, characteristically repays their friendship with scorn.

But more than unreciprocated good will is in play here. From a cautionary anecdote about the masculine haughtiness figured in the Buckel hump, Bryant shifts to the house and the red oak that shelters it as symbols of maternal indulgence and nourishment. Walter's son Caspar, whose carroty red hair suggests an affinity with the tree, shies from his strict father's regimen and finds a refuge from chores in the oak's cradling boughs. This symbolic relationship is further elaborated in Caspar's terror as powerful storms pound the tree, causing a rain of acorns that calls to mind a mother's weeping in a fierce domestic quarrel. Significantly, the onset of Caspar's puberty coincides with his father's decision to forsake the log dwelling for a new house by the side of a heavily trafficked, commercial highway and, for no logical reason, to chop down the red oak. When Caspar pleads, successfully, for the tree's life, he not only acts as this "mother's" protector but also rejects his autocratic father's crass materialism.

Bryant reinforces the association of mother and tree through a crone who has nurtured the boy's imagination with fantastic stories while he was growing up. An echo of the story's opening justification for exciting ventures into the supernatural, the old woman's evocations of monsters teach that these figures of life's menacing aspects can be dealt with if confronted; the stories serve to prepare for adulthood. Caspar enters that next stage with the crone's death (which coincides with the Buckels taking up residence in the new house), followed by the death of his parents. His reality has changed: the world, suddenly, takes notice of the boy–and it mocks him cruelly. Worst of all, the nubile Teutonic beauty who has ignited the youth's passion answers it with scorn. His mortified retreat to the red oak at that point manifests a wish to return to the protection of childhood and maternal solace.

What has been implicit now becomes virtually explicit: in the tree's rustle, he hears a human voice–obviously the old woman's– instructing him, like a doting mother, "Wash thy hands and face in the little pool in that rivulet, and go thy way home." But the water signifies more than a simple cleansing: in effect, it is a ritual, a baptism signaling rebirth in a new stage of life.* The hump that had been the emblem identifying him as his father's son miraculously subsides, planing out into the muscular, well-proportioned body of a mature, handsome young man. The ugly duckling has become a swan. A change in personality complements his physical alteration. In place of his wary, socially backward, awkward former self emerges a charming, engaging, athletic fellow of abundant good will. Female hearts are set aflutter–including that of the *zaftig* maiden who had previously rejected his suit but who now rejoices in being chosen as his bride.

---

* In "The Rivulet," a poem he had published two years earlier, a brook on the Bryant property in Cummington served as a trope for life's passage–similar to its meaning in this story. The same trope would recur in "The Stream of Life" (1845), as well as in "An Evening Revery" and a number of other poems.

Where a formulaic fairy tale would end happily with marriage, Bryant braids a darker continuation. Unused to the ways of society, Caspar squanders his inheritance, sinks into debt, and, obeying "a kind of instinct," again finds himself under the great oak's boughs. Instead of expressing gratitude for his rescue from deformity, he curses his benefactor, blaming the good looks she bestowed on him as the cause of his impoverishment. That instant, the spirit appears. She exhibits "the same calm features of unearthly loveliness and youth, with a smile playing about the beautiful mouth"; invitingly, "on each side of her face flowed down a profusion of light brown hair, that played softly in the wind." This time Bryant portrays her, not as a mother reminding her child to wash (or to acknowledge, ritualistically, having come of age), but as a sensual woman guiding a lover. She tells him to use his spade (patently phallic)in a place she points to under her trunk to find what "will suffice thy wishes," and then, as if to hide the awful secret of the act he has performed, to take care to replace the earth he disturbed. What Caspar discovers that should suffice his wishes is a pot full of gold coins, but the description of the youth's rhythmic digging in the "strong gleam of twilight," with the "boughs and foliage moving and murmuring in the night-wind" has an unmistakably erotic resonance that intimates the covert meaning of the treasure.

What is given in love is not received in wisdom, however, and Caspar, driven to purchase friendship and respect, dissipates the gold and then exhausts his credit. Once more, he contritely visits the red oak; once more he is directed to dig–in transparently sexual terms, "between the two roots that diverge eastward from my trunk"–and then to replace the turf. Once more, he retrieves a cache of coins equal to the first. And once more his reckless spending plunges him into crushing debt. The compulsive pattern of course underscores Caspar's dependency, but it also suggests a need to be punished for the guilt implied through Bryant's unmistakably sexual language.

In his final recursion to the oak, Caspar no longer begs for mercy; maddened by his ineptness, he means to pillage– and, symbolically, to assert power in a destructive act that is tantamount to rape. After his servants, at his directions, dig all about the roots without discovering a single coin, they abandon the site without observing the ritualistic tender replacement of the earth around "mother's" roots. A drought further weakens the tree, and when that damage is followed by a heavy rain, the gentle brook in which Caspar once baptized his new self swells into a torrent that excavates what remains of the supporting turf. Thus undermined–almost literally– by the effects of Caspar's violations of the spirit's love, the oak falls in a gust of wind.

The red oak's death also marks the end of her creature, the handsome Caspar: his hump reappears and he reverts to the deformed Caspar. On his return home, no one recognizes him. His black servant looses the dogs, driving the frightened (and no less frightening) fellow into the dark woods–the abode of those ghastly beasts that the crone had leashed through her tales.

In the finale, Bryant lightens the story with a touch characteristic of Irving. Caspar's wife sought her husband for half a year, he tells us, and after concluding he had died, she mourned him for another half year. But, the proprieties having been observed, life goes on: she then married a New England youth "who had fallen in love with her plump, round face, and well stocked farm." It is not the wife's fate, however, but the superseded husband's that brings the tale's meaning to completion. Bryant reports as fact that Caspar did indeed vanish without a trace, yet he adds that "the old people," believers in superstition, say he haunts the woods, running "into gloomy thickets as soon as your eye falls on him, as if to avoid the sight of man."

Naively construed, the ending has Caspar a fool, fittingly punished for profligacy and greed: if he has left no sign of his existence, it is because he has failed to become fully human. But alternative inter-pretations beg for consideration. If he is hiding from his fellow man because of shame, the gloomy thickets correspond to the unresolved Oedipal tangle in his psyche. Yet another reading hinges on perceiving the final words, "as if to avoid the sight of man," not as the protagonist's consciousness of his own guilt but as a judgment on mankind. In this view, Caspar is merely a victim. After all, the hump that isolates him from society is inherited, not the result of his deeds, and the jeers he suffers from the "good people" reflect ill of them, not of him. Similarly, the community's subsequent changed behavior toward the handsome Caspar proceeds from nothing more than his altered appearance; this impugns their character, not his. Indeed, with the single, conspicuous exception of the crone, no one who deals with Caspar shows anything other than predatory instincts. The worst of these is a schoolmaster turned merchant who, posing as a friend, entices the emotionally needy social novice to purchase every gewgaw he sells, and then, when his victim is bankrupt, shows him the door. And the rest of the community is no less willing to take advantage of his largesse. Caspar ends his engagement with society as a pariah, but Bryant simultaneously portrays those who carry on the business of life at which Caspar has failed as exploiters–including that New England youth to whom we give our approving smile as he annexes Caspar's wife and property.

Are the ambivalences in Bryant's fable a mark of sophistication, or of carelessness? Is the psychosexual element an unintended product of borrowing from similar material in various folk tales, or an intuitive expression of the unconscious? Some questions can only be left to speculation, but there is no reason to hold Bryant to a stricter test of calculation than we might apply to any other writer of his time. That he is already an artist with a sure hand in this initial venture is evident, however. His easy style and control of nuance exhibit a deliberateness in his prose that reflects the same measured qualities in his poetry. Had he gone on to write another half dozen stories of the same type–perhaps discovering what peculiar qualities he could refine and extend for his idiosyncratic purposes–he might have contributed a distinctive chapter in the history of the American short story. Instead, although his attraction to legends involving the supernatural persisted, he never attempted another variation of the classic folk tale.

Editorial responsibilities with the short-lived *United States Review and Literary Gazette* in 1826, followed during the next year by his acceptance of the assistant editorship of the *New-York Evening Post* and his series of lectures on poetry before the Athenæum Society, dampered the flow of Bryant's verses. Even so, he did not turn his back on fiction. Much like "A Pennsylvania Legend," his second story, "A Border Tradition," was born of exigency: it nicely filled many blank pages in an 1826 number of the *Gazette*, when the magazine's treasury was too strained to pay contributors. After an extensive description of nature in a settlement where Dutch and English families rub close, the author tells of an English lad's wooing and then losing interest in a young Dutch woman. The tale concludes with all being rapidly set right by the woman's sister, who, pretending to be a ghost, frightens the former suitor into renewing his lapsed affections and marrying. The echo of "The Legend of Sleepy Hollow" is unmistakable, not only in its subject matter and setting but also in its presentation as narrative (there are just six short lines of dialogue, clustered in a portion of one page).

Notwithstanding the flaccid performance in "A Border Tradition," Bryant did not lose confidence in his ability to produce creditable stories, and his close friends more than encouraged him to continue. Writing fiction evolved into a means of enjoying a robust camaraderie as they met across the Hudson at Robert Sands's Hoboken home to trade ideas for stories and critique each other's work. *The Talisman* for 1828, a gift annual assembled in 1827 for the Christmas market, contained three Bryant stories–two of them devised in collaboration with Sands and Gulian Verplanck. Good sales led to a *Talisman* for 1829, containing one Bryant tale, and a final *Talisman* the next year, to which he contributed three stories, despite having assumed the duties of editor-in-chief of the *Evening Post*. Among these was "The Indian Spring," not only his finest achievement in prose but also one deserving recognition as among the most notable American works of fiction in the first third of the nineteenth century.

The idea of one civilization succeeding another in the same place had intrigued him at least from the time he conceived "The Ages"; as an American he focused on the European displacement of Indian societies with both fascination and guilt. "The Indian Spring," though only one of several works to emerge from that conflicted interest, employs the concept most forcefully. Deceptively simple, it seems little more than a piece modeled on one of Mr. Spectator's accounts of Sir Roger de Coverley or on something Oliver Goldsmith might have written for *The Bee*, it is in fact quite artfully engineered.

Bryant starts with his narrator's recollection of having "elsewhere intimated that I have great sympathy with believers in the super-natural," but this allusion to the opening of "A Pennsylvania Legend" serves a different purpose: there, it was intended to justify a departure from realism; here, it challenges the reader to resolve whether the supernatural being about to enter the narrator's account is real or imaginary. In effect, he addresses the reading audience as an unseen jury, preparing them– *i.e.*, us–to weigh the evidence in the testimony which will follow. But this presentation is sleight of hand. Despite Bryant's doling out clues to the reader, the tale is not about solving the puzzle of whether the Indian is real. That question merely distracts attention until the reader eventually realizes he has been led to discover the Indian's dramatic, underlying relationship to the narrator.

The narrative begins in circumstances that emphasize genteel behavior and order. Two strolling companions engaged in conversation are compared in terms of corpulence; they impress us as virtual country squires. No necessary purpose motivates their walk–pointedly called a "ramble"–and although the narrator states that he carries a gun, the weapon serves only as a pretext. Killing game at the onset of winter, he soft-heartedly reasons, might spare the animals the hardship of winter, or even starvation, but depriving wildlife of their "sunny months of frolic and plenty" would offend him as "gratuitous cruelty." Nothing threatens the peace in these woods filled with the warbling of birds. The first wildlife the narrator actually sees is a red newt, and he calmly naps beside the timid creature.

The savage figure he encounters at the Indian Spring is the gentle-manly narrator's opposite in every way. This is no Jemmy Sunkum, the short, fat, drunken vagrant who is the only Indian left in the area–the rest, a boy tells the narrator, having "gone to the west'ard" since "before father came into the country–long before." The majestic apparition serves as the avatar of his dispossessed race, and his eyes accusingly "ray out an unpleasant brightness from their depths, like twin stars of evil omen," driving the narrator deeper into the forest, as though back in time to a world in which he is as utterly alien as the apparition is in the narrator's reality. Bryant underscores the division: as soon as the narrator steps back onto cleared land "sown with European grasses," the menace vanishes, and he realizes that the pursuing specter "could only haunt its ancient wilderness, and was excluded from every spot reclaimed and cultivated by the white man."

Repeatedly, the Indian appears whenever the narrator resumes his walk in the forest and vanishes when his prey steps onto a field–and the faster the narrator runs, the faster the distance from his pursuer shortens. It is not only time that is inconstant but space as well. As panic increases his body heat, he sheds his clothes and then his gun, the symbol of both his own power and of his technologically advanced civilization. Fear literally strips him of what has furnished his identity; he devolves, as it were, toward the near-naked state of the Indian. Simultaneously, the Indian dons each discarded piece of clothing, and finally picks up the firearm; step by step, he "becomes" the white man.

Had Bryant's use of the double stopped here, "Indian Spring" would stand as an early example of American literature's reliance on the device to focus on race in illustrating a humanistic moral. (Melville's Ishmael, figuratively and literally bound to his "twin" Queequeg, is one prominent instance; Twain, an author captivated by the possibilities of the double, provides another in *Pudd'nhead Wilson.*) But Bryant drives the conceit to a different consummation. As the chase approaches its inevitable end, the narrator suddenly realizes that he has circled back to where his adventure began, and, for no reason other than to under-score the author's symbolic intent, he leaps "to the very spot where I had been reposing, and where the pressure of my form still remained on the grass." In that very instant, the Indian also leaps toward the same spot and seizes him. The two figures are not just, in some sense, brothers; they are the same man, and their collision, a devastating shock of self-awareness, produces "an interval of insensibility." When the narrator regains consciousness, he is being shaken awake by the friend with whom he had begun his ramble. Had it all been only a dream? The friend "flippantly" asserts that it was, and the narrator, "when in a philosophical mood," accepts this explanation. Yet the sensations had been so real, he says, "I find nothing in them which should lead me to class them with the illusions of sleep, and nothing to distinguish them from the waking experiences of my life."

Similar self-encounters are scattered across several major works of American short fiction. Philip Roth's mid-twentieth-century story, "Eli, the Fanatic," presents a roughly correlative case. The eponymous protagonist—a suburban, Americanized Jew—is enlisted to mitigate the embarrassment his neighbors feel because a recently-arrived, Old World teacher at the *schul* refuses to shed the green clothes of the ghetto. The final scene reveals the teacher wearing Eli's cast-off Ivy League outfit, while Eli, having suffered at least momentary mental derangement, dons the teacher's history-drenched clothes—thereby embracing an identity he had sought to efface. A still more trenchant parallel occurs in Henry James's "The Jolly Corner," where a cat-and-mouse game through an old family house (corresponding to the forest and field pursuit in "The Indian Spring") leads Spencer Brydon to confront the ghostly self he would have become had he stayed in New York instead of residing in Europe. Brydon, like Bryant's narrator, faints. When his fiancée wakes him, she assures him that she would have loved this potential Brydon—horrifying as he is to himself—as much as the actual one. The most instructive comparisons, however, arise from two writers who were Bryant's contemporaries: Nathaniel Hawthorne and Edgar Allan Poe. Brown's walk into the forest in "Young Goodman Brown"–during which he meets a devil who looks, successively, like himself, like his father, and like his grandfather–takes him to a coven of the people he had previously thought "good." There he sees his wife Faith, about to join the fellowship of the wicked, and with this shattering of his innocence, it presumably dawns on him that he is himself the "nice young man to be taken into communion to-night." Self-encounter is shown as no less spoliative in "William Wilson"–in which Poe assigned the eponymous protagonist his own birth date and sent him to the very school he had attended in England. Harassed, he believes, by a new student with the same name and features but with perfect moral character, the evil Wilson finally stabs his double and hears, "In me didst thou exist–and, in my death, see by this image, which is thine own, how utterly thou hast murdered thyself." But perhaps the more telling–though more subtle–analogue is found in Poe's "The Murders in the Rue Morgue," where the hyperintellectual detective Dupin enters the mind and instincts of an ape–effectively his brutish double–to recreate the extremely violent murders.

"The Indian Spring" foreshadows the Philip Roth story in that the Indian, like the "Greenie," reflects guilt in the consideration of one's identity, but it bears a more radical relation to the other examples cited above. Despite their salient differences as writers, James, Hawthorne, and Poe express in these stories a basic idea manifested persistently and with great variety in their works: that a primal inner self–an ape, as it were, whether evil or merely monstrous–lurks beneath the orderly, civilized surface of social conduct. It is this vision that Herman Melville, in praising *Mosses from an Old Manse*, recognized as Hawthorne's "power of blackness"–and that a procession of critics has ever since remarked is a distinguishing factor in the American literary imagination. The transit of "The Indian Spring," from the bonhomie and the tender codes of humane conduct so fastidiously professed in its opening paragraphs to the narrator's clash with the dark part of his being that overwhelms his consciousness at the end, is among the earliest displays of a key tropism of our national literature.

Why did Bryant, a champion of literary nationalism who had called for the propagation of an American novel, not invest a more sustained effort of his own in writing fiction? To be sure, during the period in which he wrote his stories, he was trying to secure his family's financial security in his posts as an editor while also nourishing the reputation he had established as a poet. Joke as he did that he wrote his stories with the quill he had pulled from the tail of a swan he captured on the Avon, its serious employment to pursue fame or fortune could never have been more than a fleeting daydream. If the crudity of more than half his plots is not persuasive evidence that he was content to be a dilettante, one could cite the variability in his subject matter and structure as a sign that he had no idiosyncratic story to develop through the refinement of his art. But that evidence may be deceptive. Even though a career as a writer of tales never beckoned as a practicable alternative, a good case can be made that the best of his ventures in fiction were indeed a most personal art.

Although a story modeled on a fairy tale seems a rather unlikely place to find autobiographical references, "A Pennsylvania Legend" reflects several elements from its author's life. Both of Bryant's parents descended from relatively patrician stock that can be seen as American equivalents to the Buckels. On his father's side, he could trace his lineage to John Alden and Priscilla Mullins, but his mother's family, the Snells, presents the stronger resemblance. The frontier Pennsylvania settlement to which the Buckels emigrate corresponds to the Berkshire hamlet of Cummington, where Ebenezer Snell had arrived in 1774, only four years after erection of the first rude house. The Buckels' move, after they achieve prosperity, from a simple cabin at the edge of the woods to a comparative manse on the verge of a highway, tallies not only with that of the Snells but also, after Dr. Peter Bryant and his young family left their small hewn-log dwelling, with their uneasy amalgamation into the Snell homestead. Walter Buckel, in his aristocratic title and demeanor, is reminiscent of Squire Snell, a cold, unpopular autocratic magistrate who took charge of his grandson's upbringing because of Peter Bryant's frequent and long absences. Caspar Buckel's affectionate, storytelling old woman clearly suggests Grandmother Snell, who would make chalk drawings on the kitchen floor to illustrate her stories, with "Old Crooktail" as Cullen's particular favorite–human in form but monstrous "with horns and cloven feet and a long tail." In "A Lifetime," written two years before his death, Bryant evoked the scene in which his boyish imagination was stirred:

There stand, in the clean-swept fireplace,
  Fresh boughs from the wood in bloom,
And the birch-tree's fragrant branches
  Perfume the humble room.

And there the child is standing
  By a stately lady's knee,
And reading of ancient peoples
  And realms beyond the sea.

The circumstances of many lives in that place and age would furnish similar parallels, of course. Yet, can it be mere coincidence that *snell* is an old term for a connecting link between a hook and the loose end of a line—*i.e.*, a form of buckle? (Bryant's passion for languages, and especially for the evolution of English, suggests otherwise.) And might the hump said to show the Buckels' superiority be the correlative to Cullen Bryant's abnormally large head? Though far from grotesque, it was unusual enough that it was offered as explanation for the boy's precociousness, and according to hearsay it was supposed, falsely, that Squire Snell had sought to shrink the outsized cranium through regular immersion in frigid water.

Chasing after personal antecedents to the details of fiction generally interests the biographer more than the critic, but here the possibility that Caspar, though no self-portrait (not even of a Freudian variety), is a species of self-doodle leads to a seductive hypothesis. More curious even than this protagonist's hump is his ambiguous nature: alternately, we respond to him as a sympathetic object of fate who wants only to be accepted and have the opportunity to enjoy a normal life, and then as an unsympathetic, intemperate, overgrown child who quite deserves his ultimate exile from society among the wood's wild creatures. He is, in a sense, his own double.

"The Indian Spring" appears to be a wholly different affair, not only in subject matter but also in its organizing idea—especially if one reads it as every commentator has: in the words of Charles Brown, Bryant's principal biographer, "an evocation in prose of the spirit of the Indians," a transposition of that same theme in several of his poems. However, once one recognizes that this ghost tale is not about the Indian but about the narrator, and that both "A Pennsylvania Legend" and "The Indian Spring" are wound on the device of a double self, a seminal similarity in these stories emerges. In the former tale, the protagonist ends where he began; in his despair he chooses a savage existence, divorcing himself from everything that could give him a social identity. In the latter, the narrator is Caspar's mirror image. From the safety of his cultivated, polite, quotidian reality, he moves in a circle, simultaneously progressing vertiginously inward, until he collides with the savage within himself. The story's coda finds the narrator restored to his conventional patterns, governed by reason in his "philosophical mood," and yet the truth he has experienced in his dream is indelible.

According to his friends and associates, Bryant, throughout his life, was a man of iron discipline. That strict self-control, however, kept a fierce temper in check. At seventeen, in a long meditative letter to a close friend, he expatiated upon the conflict in man's dual nature: wisdom does not purge meanness of spirit. "The government of passion," not the quest for knowledge, ought to be paramount.

> Of what benefit is it that the understanding and imagination should be cultivated when the heart, the fountain of all noble and infamous actions, lies, like a garden covered with weeds whose rank luxuriance chokes even the plants natural to the soil. — Learning only points to the easier gratification of our sensualities and teaches us to conceal our passions, only to give them vent when the shackles of law and disgrace are removed.

That drear awareness of the brute self persisted—concealed though it was by his sober mien and James Russell Lowell's famous thumbnail portrait of him "as dignified, / As a smooth, silent iceberg, that never is ignified." Then, in 1831, a little more than a year after he wrote "The Indian Spring," the iceberg flamed in an astonishing public display.

A toast at a political dinner had cited Bryant's newspaper for "stupidity and vulgarity," and in printing the slur Bryant attributed it to William Stone, a rival editor. Stone privately assured Bryant that he had no knowledge of who had made the toast, but Bryant would not accept his word. A second denial met the same fate, whereupon Stone "branded" his accuser a liar, "if a blister can be raised on brass." The sequence of events in the subsequent confrontation of the two men on Broadway is in dispute. Bryant claimed he first cried out Stone's name; Stone insisted he was attacked from behind without warning. What witnesses agree upon is that Bryant removed a cowhide whip he had coiled inside his hat and flailed his adversary, and that Stone answered with a bamboo cane that shattered, baring a sword with which he then dueled against Bryant's horsewhip. Reports of the scandalous incident spread quickly. The next day, Bryant, not yet altogether repentant, published "an apology to society for having, in this instance taken the law into my own hands."

Rage cooled into embarrassment, then into meditation, and from that reflective pause came "Medfield," a narrative of moral example he published in his miscellany, *Tales of the Glauber Spa*. A curious piece, its frame mirrors that of "The Indian Spring." Again, two friends take a walk through the woods, and the author emphasizes their civility and tender sensibilities. When the narrator yields to instinct and kills a squirrel with his firearm, Medfield asks what he will do with the remnant of a life needlessly taken. When the narrator goes fishing, his companion rebukes him for torturing the worm on his hook. Medfield's saintliness even extends to those who revile him without justification: after replying to a burst of epithets with serenity, he comments to the narrator, "I only wish that the composure with which I hear his opinion of me did not irritate him so much." His friend marvels at his unnatural disposition, but Medfield insists his nature is like that of other men. What changed his behavior was the death of his beloved daughter, who would tremble at his "stern moods," and his subsequent promise to his dying wife when she asked him to overcome "that severity and impetuosity of temper which make you less useful and less beloved in the world than the qualities of your mind and heart would otherwise make you." Medfield then recites a series of provocations in which her ghostly hand has restrained him from violent acts of reprisal.

Platitudinous and flatly presented, the story is entirely negligible except in one respect: the similarity between the main character and the author. Medfield resembles Bryant, not only physically (including gray eyes, "a finely arched forehead," and the thinned "light brown hair that curled over it") but also in his knowledge of rare plants, his "rational" interest in politics and religion, and his service as a magistrate (Bryant had held a minor judicial office while practicing law in Great Barrington). They share an unusual degree of competence in foreign and ancient literatures, an expert familiarity with Old English, and a love of ballads–and both can recite James Thomson's long poem "The Seasons" from memory. Still more telling is the resonance of the narrative's critical event, which precipitated his dedication to peace. Although Medfield's loss of wife and daughter does not precisely match the author's life, Bryant's favorite sibling, Sarah, whom he described as exceptionally meek, died five years before he wrote the story—corresponding to the time of Medfield's bereavement. Perhaps the most intriguing link, however, emerges in the story's final words: gratuitously, the narrator informs the reader that Medfield died in June, "aged 36"–Bryant's own age in the very month he wrote "Medfield."

To what is this a clue? That "Medfield" comments on the self's terrifying underside in "The Indian Spring" seems obvious, but just as significant is that it punctuates a succession of narratives coiled around terror: "Adventure in the East Indies," about a tiger hunt (1827); "A Story of the Island of Cuba," a blood-soaked account of vengeance and of tracking the murderers (1829); and "The Skeleton's Cave," where three trapped men contemplate cannibalism before their rescue (1829). Even though Bryant's poems sometimes confront death and suffering, and, rarely, introduce murder or ruthless acts, he was not a poet who searched the psychological dimensions of violence or fear–that complex territory was left to his prose "rambles," a freer endeavor because both author and audience regarded it so much less seriously. "Medfield," however, put an end to such veiled explorations: he never again attempted fiction. The Stone incident had brought to the surface impulses that owed their fascination to the obligation to hide and abhor them; in the open, he could only renounce them. Once Medfield had served as his vehicle for that abnegation, it was time to bury the conflicted self he represented.

After "The Prairies," inspired by a trip to Illinois to see his brother after publishing *Tales of the Glauber Spa*, Bryant's poetry tended steadily downward from the level of his first decade of printed poems. But it can also be said that none of his post-1832 poems rivals "The Indian Spring." Later, while the Civil War's carnage grieved a divided nation, Bryant reverted to storytelling in several sentimental, long narrative poems in emulation of Lowell and Longfellow, who had eclipsed his own popularity. Neither the magic slippers that draw a maid to consort with the nymphs in the watery realm of "Sella" nor the child-like ethereal beings of death who summon Eva in "The Little People of the Snow," however, express more than a gentle seduction to surrender life. The fragile superficiality of these fables only accentuates the loss in his failure, decades earlier, to pursue a path of greater promise that led from deeper recesses of his psyche.